THE ATOM

Fundamental Physics I

Marshall Cavendish Books, London W1

Marshall Cavendish Books Limited
58, Old Compton Street, London W1

First published 1969
© Marshall Cavendish Limited 1968
© Marshall Cavendish Books Limited 1969

Printed by Proost, Turnhout, Belgium
462 00620 4

Contents

Introduction
by K. F. Smith

Professor of Experimental Physics, University of Sussex

THE WORD 'Atom' comes from the Greek word 'Atomos', which means "that which cannot be cut". An ancient Greek philosopher first proposed that matter might consist of empty space containing very small particles, invisible, indivisible, indestructible, inpenetrable and eternal, and that everything is associated with the positions, sizes, shapes and motions of 'atoms'. Experimental support for this concept did not come until scientists in the eighteenth century had carried out the work which led Dalton to publish his famous atomic theory in 1808, thereby initiating physical science as we think of it today. We still believe that matter is composed of atoms, but our picture of an atom is very different from Dalton's.

This book contains an account of the experiments carried out in the last 300 years, most of them in this century, to determine the structure of the atom and the relationship between atomic and nuclear structure and electro-magnetic radiations such as radio-waves, light waves, x-rays and gamma-rays. It has turned out to be much more complicated than the early scientists believed, the fundamental entities seem to be particles such as the protons, electrons, neutrons from which the atoms are built, rather than the atoms themselves. Newton's laws have been replaced by the laws of quantum mechanics to account for the behaviour of particles and electro-magnetic waves on an atomic scale and the development of both the theory and experiment in the last 50 years has already revolutionized not only the world of science but also our everyday life. There is no doubt that protons attract electrons, and we can explain the general nature of such electrostatic forces in terms of an exchange of photons, the particles which we normally associate with electro-magnetic radiations. In the same way we relate nuclear forces to the exchange of other fundamental particles, the mesons, many of which have now been discovered. It is a mysterious world of invisible particles, no longer indivisible or indestructible. A significant proportion of the world's scientific effort is at present devoted to the solution of the problem of the origin of the fundamental particles.

The atom that isn't

Atom, from the Greek word *atomos*, means 'that which cannot be cut'. It has proved something of a misnomer. Yet the atom remains one of the most fruitful of scientific ideas. Where did it spring from?

SOME 2,400 YEARS ago, a young Greek philosopher, Zeno of Elea, insisted that it was impossible to shut a door. Say the door has to move three feet, he argued. Before it can shut it must cover half that distance. Before it can cover half it must cover a quarter. And so on *ad infinitum*. But how can a body possibly cross an infinite number of distances in a finite time? A closing door must obviously be an illusion and the same must apply to all motion and change. Reality must be one, immovable and continuous.

The point to notice is that the Eleatics, the school of philosophers to which Zeno belonged and gave his name, started from logical and mathematical ideas in their attempts to describe reality. Distrusting their senses they chose not to rely on observation, and their paradoxes lent intellectual weight to the 'common-sense' supposition that matter – a lump of lead for example – was perfectly solid and, in theory at any rate, infinitely divisible.

Only atoms and empty space

About 420 BC, another Greek philosopher, Democritus, who taught at Abdera in Thrace, tried to explain why various substances differed in density. His assertion that less dense substances had more 'open spaces' inside them, led him to conclude that matter was not continuous but

made of 'pieces'. Moreover, though he too mistrusted the 'bastard evidence' of his senses, he found motion and change convincingly real and pointed out that there can be no movement without space to move in. Borrowing the Eleatic notion of the eternal oneness of reality, he described the 'pieces' making up the world of matter as invisible, indivisible, indestructible, impenetrable and eternal. Everything is merely an effect of the positions, sizes, shapes and motions of atoms. 'Only atoms and empty space exist,' he said, 'all else is superficial appearance.' (Democritus probably owed many of his ideas to Leucippus of Miletus, who is said to have lived *c.* 450 BC – though Leucippus' existence was denied by Epicurus, another Greek philosopher, who championed the atomism of Democritus *c.* 300 BC.)

But without experimental support, atomism was still little more than one bold idea among several. Unfortunately Aristotle (384–322 BC), the most influential of all Greek philosophers, rejected out of hand the notion that matter was discontinuous and lent his authority to the view of the philosopher Empedocles (*c.* 450 BC) that all material things were composed of four elements – earth (a solid), water (a liquid), air (a gas) and fire (an intangible element), combined in varying proportions. It was this speculative theory of matter that was to dominate thinking throughout the Middle Ages and give rise to the tradition of alchemy. Many alchemists – particularly the earlier ones – were dedicated investigators of the properties of matter, but for nearly 2,000 years they made virtually no progress in their efforts to understand the ways in which various substances are related. The four-element theory was simply accepted as an article of faith. It did not rest on any basis of experimental proof and there was no obvious way of testing it. The alchemist's energies were dissipated by the need to explain the phenomena he observed in the philosophical language of Empedocles and Aristotle – a task requiring considerable ingenuity. Gradually investigators began to distinguish between the *general* problem of accounting for change in the world and the *concrete* problem of explaining actual changes in things.

Alchemy loses ground

The Englishman, Robert Boyle (1627–91), was the first to break away decisively from the four-element theory and fasten his allegiance on the experimental rather than the metaphysical. Although, like his younger contemporary, Isaac Newton, he was never quite able to free himself from the fascination of alchemy, he sympathized with the atomism of Democritus (interest in which had been stimulated in 1649 by the French clergyman, Pierre Gassendi, in an appendix to a book on Epicurus' philosophy). Elements, in Boyle's view, were 'simple bodies of matter which cannot be resolved into other bodies of matter and of which all other bodies of matter are composed'. Unfortunately this definition was still unscientific, for Boyle – and he fully appreciated the difficulty – had no way of bearing it out experimentally. Isaac Newton (1642–1727), like Boyle, also knew where the future lay. 'First to enquire diligently into the properties of things, and of establishing these proper-

A blind alley. The alchemists' attempts to turn lead into gold and discover the 'elixir of life' were based on reasonings unaided by observation.

Order in apparent chaos. A corner of Lord Rutherford's laboratory at Cambridge where it was shown that the atom is not indivisible after all.

Less personal, more functional, the design of this tidy laboratory reflects the meticulous planning demanded by modern scientific research.

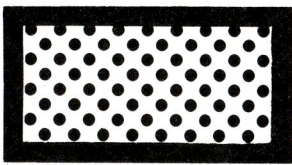

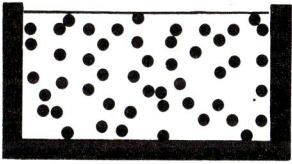

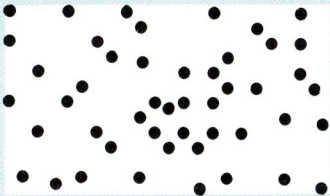

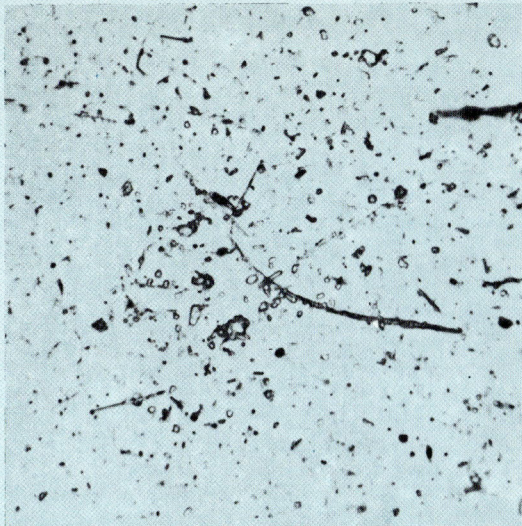

A solid, a liquid and a gas, *left, top to bottom*. A theory of atoms makes it easier to understand how ice melts and water boils. Dust in a shaft of sunlight, *above*, may have prompted early ideas about atoms.

ties by experiment, and then to proceed more slowly to hypotheses for the explanation of them.' At last, the horse was being put before the cart.

A pair of scales argues for atoms

The path from metaphysical atomism to scientific atomic theory was paved by the French chemist Antoine Lavoisier (1743–94), beheaded during the French Revolution. In his hands, a simple but accurate weighing mechanism, the chemical balance, began to unlock the secrets of matter. For the first time, relationships between substances in chemical reactions began to be expressed in mathematical form. Lavoisier discovered that the weight of a new substance (tin oxide, a compound of tin and oxygen) formed when tin is strongly heated in air trapped in an inverted jar, invariably equalled the weight of the original tin plus the weight lost by the air (its oxygen content). This experiment became the foundation of the first and most basic quantitative law in chemistry, the *Law of Conservation of Mass*[1] –

that there is no loss of weight (or, rather, mass) during chemical change.

Carrying out similar experiments, chemists soon found themselves in a position to formulate a second law, the *Law of Definite Proportions*. This law states that when two pure substances combine to form a given compound, they do so in definite proportions by weight. The Law of Definite Proportions was to prove the first truly scientific clue to the existence of atoms, and it was seized upon by an English schoolmaster, John Dalton (1766–1844), the founder of atomic theory.

Dalton began his career of an amateur in chemistry by studying gases and was greatly struck by the way in which they can be converted first into liquids and then into solids by varying certain conditions – increasing pressure and decreasing temperature. Clearly a gas was somehow a

[1] *Weight* unlike *mass* is dependent on variations in the pull of gravity. Mass is the 'constant weight' of a substance relative to other substances under the same gravitational conditions.

DEMOCRITUS   LUCRETIUS   NEWTON

DALTON   KELVIN   RUTHERFORD

Six great champions of the atom. Democritus, Lucretius and Newton span 2,000 years of speculation; Dalton, Kelvin and Rutherford could support their theories with experimental proof.

dispersed solid, and the atomism of the ancients again strongly recommended itself as a possible explanatory model. Dalton brought this model to bear upon the Law of Definite Proportions and discovered that the law was suddenly illuminated. He saw that the law could have meaning only if each element were made up of separate particles all having the same weight. Take pure water, for example, a simple compound of the elements hydrogen and oxygen. No matter how many samples of whatever volume are analysed, the weight ratio of oxygen to hydrogen always turns out to be the same – eight to one. Invariable ratios also occur in other compounds – even in cases where one element combines with another, giving several different weight ratios. If, in these latter cases, the weight of one of the elements is standardized, that is, made the same in each case, the weights of the other element will be in simple ratios to each other. For example, under certain conditions, copper and oxygen will combine to form two different compounds. But analysis of these compounds shows that if the weight of copper is made the same in both cases, the weights of oxygen will stand in a ratio to each other of two to one. This and similar experiments led Dalton to formulate the *Law of Multiple Proportions* which states that a simple ratio must hold between the two weights of one element that can combine with a given weight of another element.

If an element in a chemical compound were not present in the form of individual particles, and if each of these particles were not of the same weight, it is most highly improbable that water and the oxides of copper would analyse as they do. That the laws of definite and multiple proportions hold good is the strongest possible evidence for the existence of atoms. Accordingly, in 1808, Dalton published his famous atomic theory in which he made the following assertions: (1) Elements consist of tiny, indivisible, indestructible particles called atoms. (2) Atoms of any given element are identical in weight; while atoms of different ele-

The man who propounded the first scientific theory of atoms, largely as a result of his study of gases, John Dalton stirs up the mud at the bottom of a pond while a young helper traps bubbles of marsh gas (methane) as they rise.

ments invariably differ in weight. (3) Atoms combine with other atoms to form the 'compound atoms' (molecules) of chemical compounds, and always do so in fixed simple ratios. (4) Atoms of different elements may combine in more than one ratio. (5) If two elements form only one known compound, the compound must be made up of only one atom of each element. The fifth of these assertions, known as the 'rule of greatest simplicity' was the hardest to accept for, unlike the others, it took matters a step farther than the experimental evidence allowed. But Dalton clung to it obstinately and insisted that water molecules consisted of only two atoms –

1

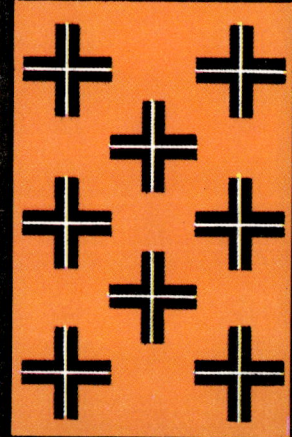

2

3

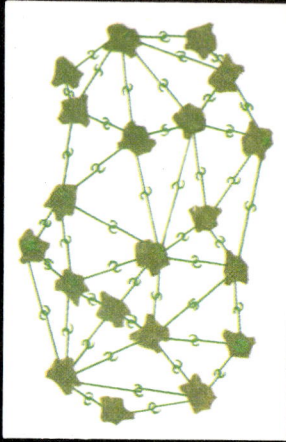

4

5

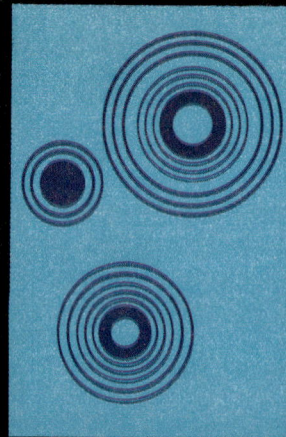

6

7

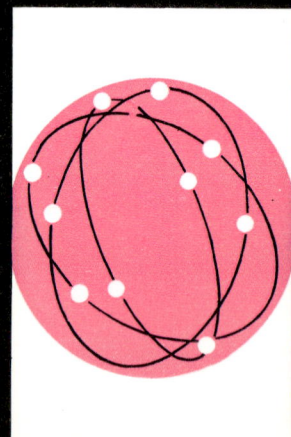

8

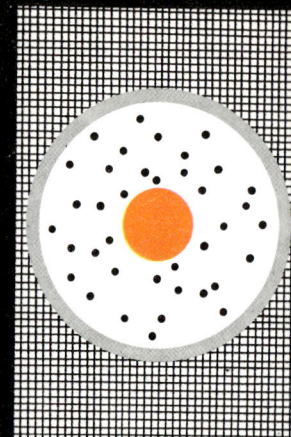

9

From atomism to atomic theory: the nine diagrams, *left*, show how key thinkers and investigators from Zeno of Elea to Rutherford may have pictured the structure of matter.

1 The common-sense view that matter is continuous and not composed of indivisible particles, was supported by the arguments of the Eleatic philosophers and approved by Aristotle.

2 The Pythagoreans thought that matter consisted of an infinite number of monads — geometrical points which in some way 'flowed' into line, surface and solid.

3 It was Leucippus and Democritus in the fifth century BC who first suggested that nothing exists except atoms in empty space.

4 Epicurus, whose philosophy is known through the work of the Latin poet, Lucretius, endorsed the new atomism. He suggested that atoms forming solids are hooked together mechanically.

5 The ancient atomism did not develop further until the seventeenth century. Sir Isaac Newton suggested that atoms are linked together by a force analogous to magnetism or gravity.

6 John Dalton pictured solid spherical atoms surrounded by atmospheres of 'caloric' or heat.

7 In the nineteenth century, Lord Kelvin visualized a ring of electricity whirling through space.

8 Sir Joseph Thomson's atom, defined early this century, was a ball of electricity studded with sub-atomic particles called electrons.

9 In 1911, Lord Rutherford stated that the atom has a heavy nucleus surrounded by electrons.

one atom of oxygen and one atom of hydrogen. As a result he ran his theory aground on a reef provided by the French chemist, Gay-Lussac (1778–1850).

Avogadro to the rescue

In experimenting with gases, Gay-Lussac had discovered that when two or more gases combine in a chemical reaction, the volumes of each of the combining gases are in the ratio of small, whole numbers. For example, he found that *two* unit volumes of hydrogen will combine with only *one* unit volume of oxygen to give *two* unit volumes of steam (gaseous water). If Dalton's view of the water molecule were correct, it would have taken *two* volumes of oxygen to produce the same result, and the painstaking Gay-Lussac, who could offer no explanation, found himself undeservedly accused of carelessness in his experiments. Others sided against Dalton and criticized his theory of atoms.

The controversy was to rage for nearly 50 years before it was finally resolved. Ironically the simple clue reconciling Dalton's theory with Gay-Lussac's observations had been published in a leading science journal in the early days of the controversy. An Italian physicist, Amadeo Avogadro (1776–1857), had seen at once that, if Gay-Lussac's observations were to support any atomic theory at all, equal volumes of gases under identical conditions of temperature and pressure must contain the *same* number of particles. And furthermore, each of these particles in the combining gases must consist of at least two atoms. Everything would fall into place if each two-atom particle of oxygen provides two pairs of hydrogen atoms with an oxygen atom apiece: $(HH)+(HH)+(OO)$ gives $(HHO)+(HHO)$.

When this solution, known as Avogadro's Hypothesis, was resurrected in 1860 by another Italian chemist, Stanislao Cannizzaro, two of Dalton's assumptions were exploded: the unwary assumption that each of the particles composing a gas consisted of a *single* atom; and the 'simplicity rule' which had led him to insist (to the point of perversity) on his formula for water (HO).

Atomic theory had been badly shaken, but had emerged purified. Said one chemist at the time: 'It was as though scales fell from my eyes.' Avogadro had exposed Dalton's weaknesses, but at the same time resoundingly re-established the scientific relevance of the atom.

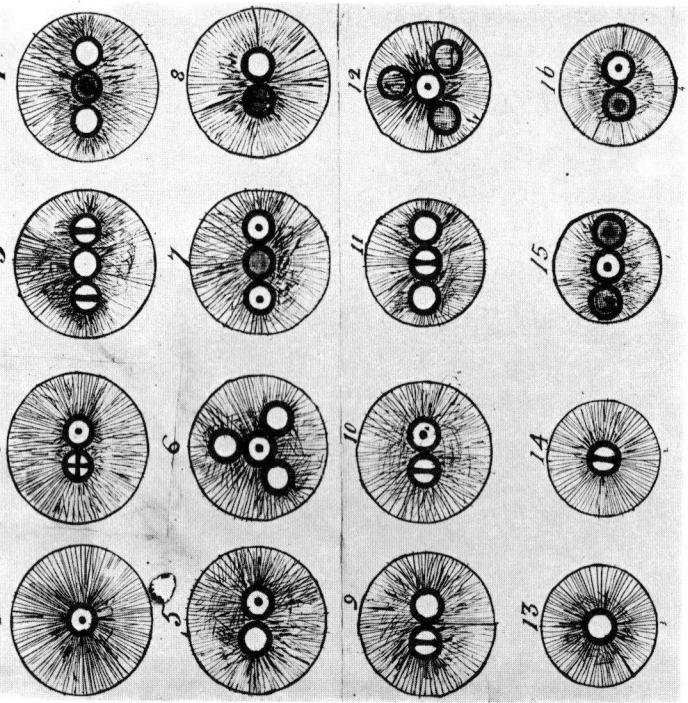

ATOMS OF ELASTIC FLUIDS

ELEMENTS.

Element	Symbol	Weight
Hydrogen.	⊙	1
Azote	⊖	5
Carbon	●	5₄
Oxygen	○	7
Phosphorus	◭	9
Sulphur	⊕	13
Magnesia	◈	20
Lime	◐	24
Soda	⊖	28
Potash	⊜	42
Strontian	⊕	46
Barytes	✳	68
Iron	Ⓘ	50
Zinc	Ⓩ	56
Copper	Ⓒ	56
Lead	Ⓛ	90
Silver	Ⓢ	190
Gold	Ⓖ	190
Platina	Ⓟ	190
Mercury	⊛	167

Dalton gave a special symbol to each element, *left*, in order to show more clearly how atoms combine to form molecules or 'compound atoms', *above*. These symbols were the forerunners of modern chemical symbols, and the diagrams of 'elastic fluids' (gases) closely resemble modern molecular diagrams. Notice that the hydrogen (1) and oxygen (13) molecules each have only one atom. Experimental evidence suggested two, but Dalton refused to reconsider.

The atom answers back

Questioned by the ingenious experiments of Thomson, Millikan and Rutherford, the atom began to reveal its plan: one or more tiny particles orbiting round a central nucleus.

LESS THAN a century ago chemists still believed that elements consisted of atoms that were indivisible homogeneous balls of matter. Dalton and Avogadro had shown that atoms combine to form molecules, although they did not understand how the combination takes place. Then in 1897, the British physicist J. J. Thomson (1856–1940) began his study of cathode rays that led to the discovery of the electron.

It was already known that if two metal plates are sealed into the ends of a glass tube from which most of the air has been pumped out, an electric current can be made to flow between the two plates or electrodes. But to carry the current, something must move along the tube between the electrodes. A small sheet of glass coated with zinc sulphide and placed inside the tube glows when the current is turned on. The glow actually consists of tiny bursts of light. It is as if particles of electricity are travelling along the tube and hitting the zinc sulphide.

By turning the zinc-sulphide screen around, Thomson showed that the stream of particles was coming out of the negatively charged electrode (cathode) and flowing to the positively charged electrode (anode). And by putting a piece of metal in the stream of particles, he got a shadow on the fluorescent zinc-sulphide screen, showing that the cathode rays travel in straight lines.

Electrons are discovered

When the rays fell on the vanes of a small paddle wheel inside the tube, the wheel turned, proving that the rays consist of particles. Thomson also found that the stream of particles was deflected by electric and magnetic fields. Since the stream was deflected towards the positive plate producing the electric field, the stream must consist of negatively charged particles. He called these negatively charged particles of electricity *electrons*.

The deflection of the stream of electrons in an electric field depends on the charge on them and on the strength of the field. In a magnetic field, which has no effect on *stationary* charged particles, the deflection depends on the strength of the field, the charge on the electron, and its velocity. Thomson arranged a cathode-ray tube with external electric and magnetic fields and he adjusted the fields to work in opposite directions so that the stream of electrons remained undeflected. From a knowledge of the strengths of the fields, he was able to calculate the ratio of the charge on an electron to its mass, e/m.

But where do the electrons come from? When the current is flowing through the cathode-ray tube, they come out of the cathode and pass into the anode. But where are they when no current is flowing? They must be in the metal that forms the electrodes and wires. But metals, and all elements, consist of atoms. Therefore electrons must come from inside atoms.

Electrons can be removed from atoms fairly easily. When a piece of amber is rubbed with fur, the amber becomes negatively charged. That is, it has a crowd of particles of negative electricity on it, a crowd of electrons. The electrons are removed from some of the atoms of the fur merely by rubbing and are deposited on the amber.

These facts suggest that all atoms contain electrons and that the electrons are probably near the surface of the atoms. But how heavy are electrons? Before Thomson discovered the electron, the lightest known particle was an atom of hydrogen with a mass of 1 on the atomic-weight scale. Since an atom of hydrogen contains at least one electron, the electron must weigh less than 1. How much less?

Thomson had measured e/m for an electron. An American physicist, Robert A. Millikan, reasoned that if he could measure the charge e, he could calculate its mass. To do this, he devised an ingenious experiment in which oil droplets were charged with an equivalent of one or two electronic charges and introduced between two horizontal metal plates connected to a source of electricity. Under the force of gravity, the droplets tended to fall towards the lower plate. By observing the rate of fall and from a relationship known as Stokes' Law, Millikan calculated the weight of the droplets. And by arranging the plates so that the top one had an opposite charge to the charge on the droplets, he could use the electric field between the plates to overcome the force of gravity and attract the droplets up-

First man to break the nucleus of an atom, Lord Rutherford. In a nitrogen-gas-filled chamber, *right*, radioactive polonium emitted a stream of alpha particles. Sometimes, a nitrogen atom absorbed an alpha particle. When this happened, the atom shed a charged hydrogen nucleus which struck a fluorescent screen at the end of the tube, producing a flash of light. Later, the process was photographed in a device known as a cloud chamber. Cutting back across the stream of alpha-particle tracks, *below*, is the path of an ejected hydrogen nucleus. As a result of this experiment, physicists worked towards the conclusion that the nuclei of all elements consist of hydrogen nuclei in greater or lesser quantities. They gave them the name *protons*.

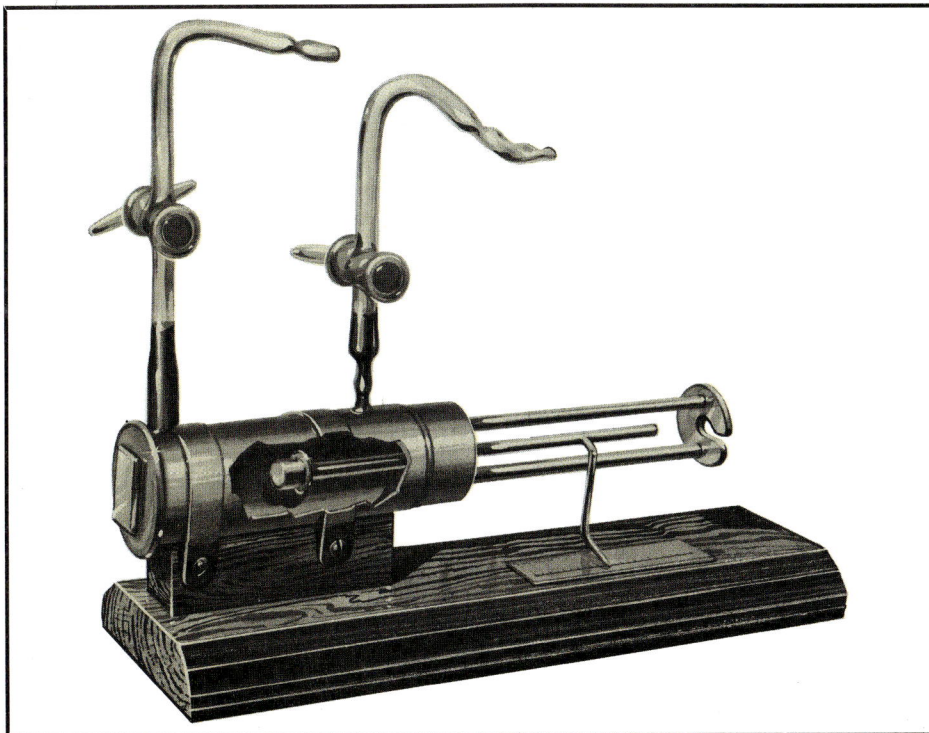

wards. By very careful control of the field, he could make the droplets remain stationary. When this happened, the upward electrical force on a droplet equalled the downward gravitational force on it and Millikan was able to calculate the charge. He found that the charge was always a small multiple of a certain quantity and this quantity was the elementary electric charge, the charge on an electron, *e*.

Combining Thomson's value for *e*/*m* and Millikan's value for *e* gives the mass of the electron as about one two-thousandth of the mass of the hydrogen atom. The remainder of an atom, which includes nearly all of its mass, must have a positive charge to balance the negative charge on the electrons.

Chemists now had to revise their ideas of the atom. They knew it consisted of one or more tiny negatively charged electrons and a comparatively large positively charged part. But how were these various parts arranged? Thomson suggested that atoms consist mainly of a positively charged jelly-like mass with the tiny electrons embedded in it. This theory was abandoned as a result of experiments made by Ernest Rutherford (1871–1937), who also used charged particles and a zinc-sulphide screen.

Rutherford used alpha particles which are given off spontaneously by the radioactive element radium. (Deflection experiments showed that alpha particles have a mass of 4 and carry two positive charges.) He directed a stream of alpha particles against a piece of thin gold foil and used the fluorescent zinc-sulphide screen to study what happened. He found that most

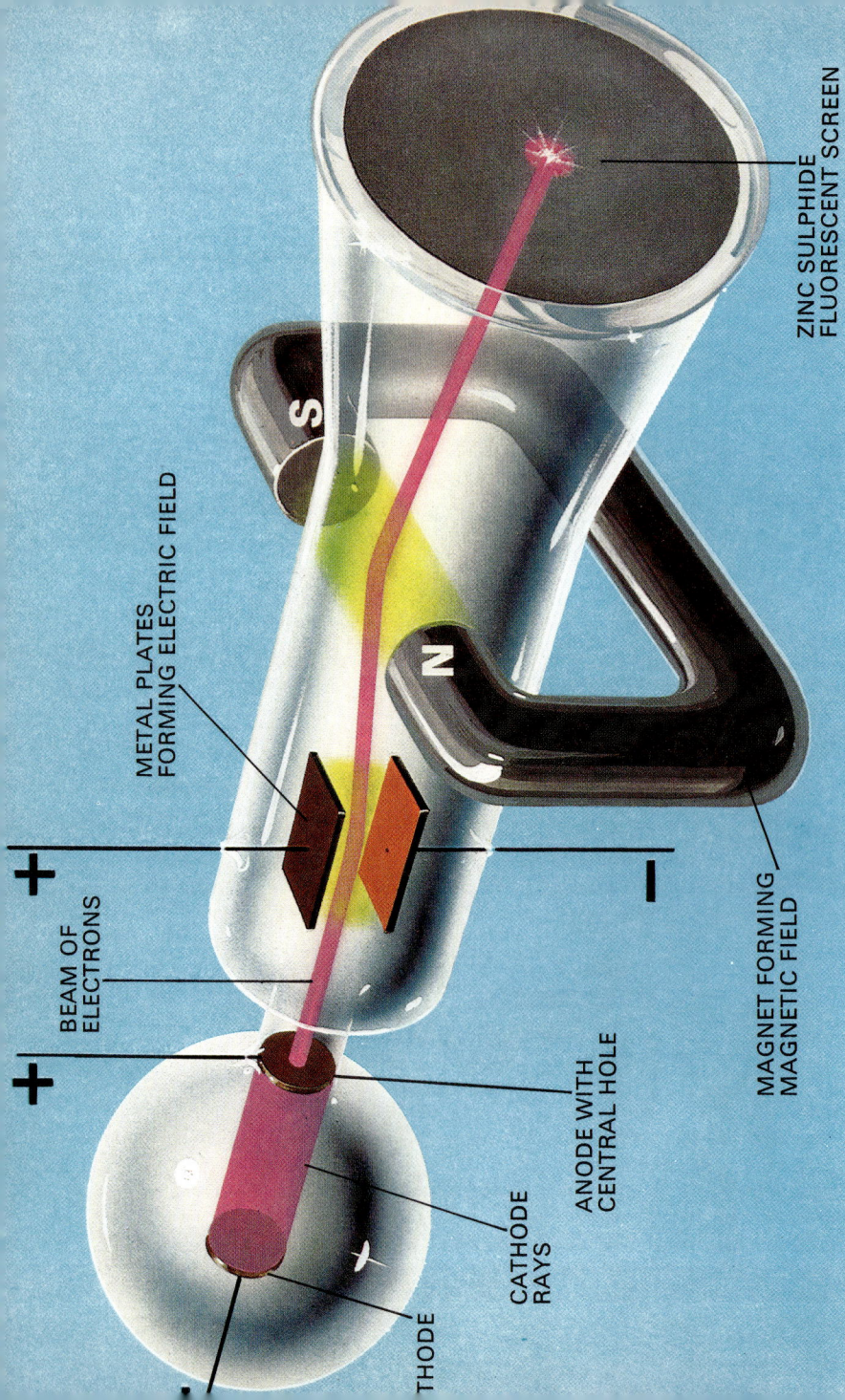

ZINC SULPHIDE
FLUORESCENT SCREEN

METAL PLATES
FORMING ELECTRIC FIELD

+

+

BEAM OF
ELECTRONS

MAGNET FORMING
MAGNETIC FIELD

ANODE WITH
CENTRAL HOLE

CATHODE
RAYS

THODE

S

N

+

–

Events in a vacuum tube enabled physicist J. J. Thomson to describe particles of electricity. He named them electrons. The particles flow from the negatively charged cathode to the anode, passing through a hole in its centre as a beam. Thomson found that the electric field (between plus and minus plates) and the magnetic field (between north and south poles) deflected the beam. Degree of deflection depends in part on the charge on the electron. By adjusting the fields, whose strength he knew, he could calculate the ratio of the charge on an electron to its mass.

of the alpha particles passed straight through the gold foil as if it were not there. Some particles were scattered as they passed through the foil, some through quite large angles even to the extent of bouncing almost directly back. Rutherford deduced that most of the gold atom must consist of empty space. An alpha particle that was scattered through a small angle was deflected as it passed very near the positively charged part of the gold atom. And an occasional alpha particle must have had a violent collision with this part of the atom and as a result bounced right back. Thus most of the mass of the gold atom and all the positive charge must be concentrated at the centre at what Rutherford called the *nucleus* of the atom.

The rest of the atom, and most of it in terms of volume, consists of a swarm of electrons. In order that the positive charge on the nucleus does not pull the negatively charged electrons into the centre of the atoms, the electrons must be moving rapidly round the nucleus, and the space containing the electrons was calculated at about ten thousand times the diameter of the nucleus.

Rutherford's model of the atom resembles the solar system. Electrons move in orbits in space a long way from the central nucleus in much the same way that the planets orbit round the sun. Hydrogen has one electron and a single positive charge on its nucleus. The hydrogen nucleus weighs very nearly 1 atomic weight unit, the weight of the whole atom. Other atoms have more electrons, with a similar number of positive charges on their nuclei. For example, carbon has six electrons and six positive charges on its nucleus. But the atomic weight of carbon is 12 – and the mass of the electrons is only six two-thousandths. In the hydrogen nucleus, *one* positive charge 'weighs' 1 unit but in the carbon nucleus, only *six* positive charges 'weigh' 12 units. In an attempt to resolve this anomaly, Rutherford in 1900, tried to break open atomic nuclei by bombarding them with streams of alpha particles.

He bombarded hydrogen atoms, and most of the alpha particles remained undeflected. But when a collision did take place, there also appeared a positively charged hydrogen nucleus. He then tried bombarding heavier elements such as nitrogen and sodium, but again he got only charged hydrogen nuclei. Rutherford had split the atomic nucleus and it began to appear that the nuclei of all elements were made up of hydrogen nuclei, which were given the name *protons*. A proton has a mass of 1 and a single positive charge. The carbon nucleus, with six positive charges, must contain six protons, which contribute 6 units to its mass. But what makes up the rest of the carbon nucleus (which has a mass of 12)? Also, since protons each weigh 1 unit, why are all atomic weights not whole numbers?

A new element

The answer to the second question was found first. The first clue came in 1906 with the discovery of a new element that was named ionium. It was found in the mineral pitchblende and its atomic weight was measured as 231·5. Another element found in pitchblende, thorium, has an atomic weight of 232·1. When chemists began to study the chemical properties of ionium, they found that they were the same as those of thorium. It appeared that there were two kinds of thorium, identical chemically but with different atomic weights. Then in 1910, Frederick Soddy suggested the complete answer. He said there *are* two kinds of thorium; both have the same number of electrons and protons (and therefore the same chemical properties) but one form has a nucleus of mass 230 and one a nucleus of mass 232. 'Ionium' and thorium are different mixtures of both forms. Soddy called the different

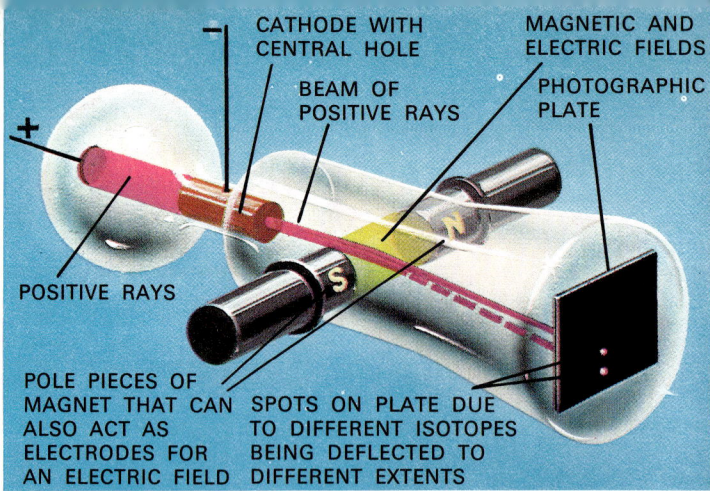

CATHODE WITH CENTRAL HOLE

MAGNETIC AND ELECTRIC FIELDS

BEAM OF POSITIVE RAYS

PHOTOGRAPHIC PLATE

POSITIVE RAYS

POLE PIECES OF MAGNET THAT CAN ALSO ACT AS ELECTRODES FOR AN ELECTRIC FIELD

SPOTS ON PLATE DUE TO DIFFERENT ISOTOPES BEING DEFLECTED TO DIFFERENT EXTENTS

New elements, identical chemically, but with differing atomic weights, puzzled scientists in the early 1900s. Could they be two kinds of the same element? J. J. Thomson, projecting neon gas ions through a tube, found that a magnetic field split the beam, deflecting a few heavier particles to a separate spot on the plate. There are, he demonstrated, two kinds, or *isotopes*, of neon.

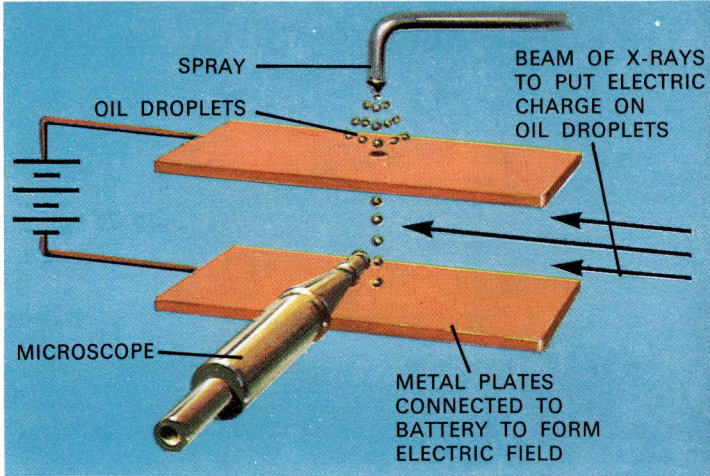

SPRAY

BEAM OF X-RAYS TO PUT ELECTRIC CHARGE ON OIL DROPLETS

OIL DROPLETS

MICROSCOPE

METAL PLATES CONNECTED TO BATTERY TO FORM ELECTRIC FIELD

Oil droplets suspended in mid-air enabled American physicist Robert A. Millikan to measure the charge on an electron (*e*). X-rays put a charge on the droplets, which tend through the force of gravity to fall. But a charge on the top plate, opposite to the charge on the droplets, counteracts the fall. Calculation on the basis of the known forces involved gives the value for *e*.

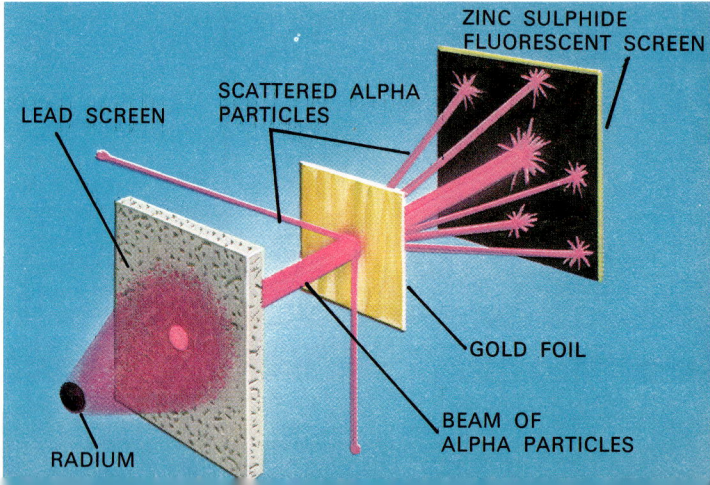

ZINC SULPHIDE FLUORESCENT SCREEN

SCATTERED ALPHA PARTICLES

LEAD SCREEN

GOLD FOIL

BEAM OF ALPHA PARTICLES

RADIUM

Before this experiment, scientists pictured the atom as a positively charged mass with electrons embedded in it. Rutherford, by firing a stream of alpha particles at a sheet of gold foil, showed that much of the atom was empty space. Some particles passed straight through the foil. Others bounced back, or were deflected. Rutherford concluded that the atom had a nucleus, orbited by an electron swarm.

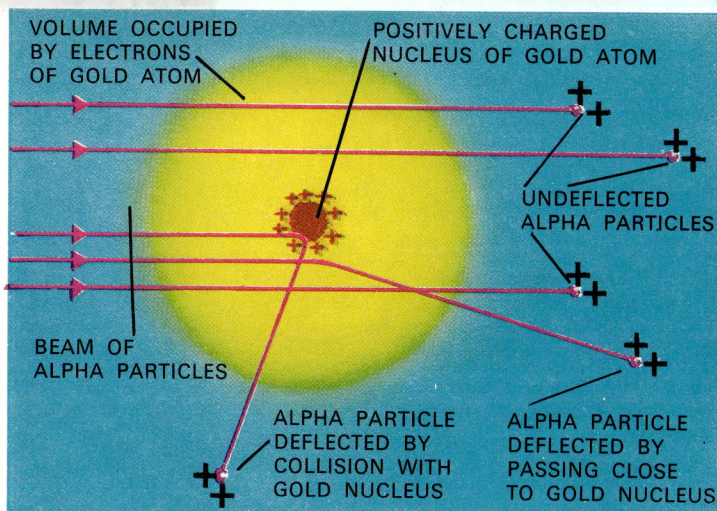

VOLUME OCCUPIED BY ELECTRONS OF GOLD ATOM

POSITIVELY CHARGED NUCLEUS OF GOLD ATOM

UNDEFLECTED ALPHA PARTICLES

BEAM OF ALPHA PARTICLES

ALPHA PARTICLE DEFLECTED BY COLLISION WITH GOLD NUCLEUS

ALPHA PARTICLE DEFLECTED BY PASSING CLOSE TO GOLD NUCLEUS

Rutherford's alpha particles took one of three paths through the gold foil. Some passed straight through, travelling in between the gold nuclei. Some, passing close to a positively charged gold nucleus, scattered — deflected off course. A few actually collided with a nucleus, bouncing back from the thin sheet of foil.

weight-forms of a single element *isotopes*.

Further evidence for the existence of isotopes was obtained by J. J. Thomson. He again used an evacuated tube with an anode and this time a thick cathode having a hole drilled through it. If, when the current is switched on, negatively charged electrons are flowing from the cathode to the anode, Thomson reasoned that some form of positive rays should be flowing from the anode to the cathode. Some of these rays would pass through the hole in the cathode and emerge as a beam that could be detected by a photographic plate. He also reasoned that the rays would consist of gas atoms that had been stripped of electrons – that is, they would be positively charged particles, the nuclei of the gas atoms. And by using a magnet to deflect the beam of positive rays (in the same way as he had deflected electron beams), Thomson was able to calculate the mass of the charged particles. Heavy particles would be deflected less than light particles. For example, with a tube containing a trace of neon gas, he got a deflection corresponding to a particle of mass 20. Neon has an atomic weight of 20·18, and Thomson had detected positive neon ions. But when he examined the photographic plate more closely, he saw another faint spot corresponding to a particle of

mass 22. There is no element of atomic weight 22 and so Thomson deduced that there are two kinds of neon, one of mass 20 and one of mass 22. Furthermore, ordinary neon is a mixture containing about 90 per cent of the lighter isotope and about 10 per cent of the heavier, giving the non-integral atomic weight of 20·18.

The neutron

The discovery of isotopes also provided evidence for the answer to our other question: what, in addition to protons, makes up the mass of the nucleus? The two isotopic forms of neon and thorium differ in mass by 2 units. It is as if there were yet a third atomic particle with unit mass but with no charge. Finally in 1932, James Chadwick also performed experiments with alpha particles. He bombarded beryllium and detected a powerful, penetrating radiation. The new rays are not deflected by thick sheets of metal nor by magnetic or electric fields, so they can have no electric charge. Occasionally, they do suffer collisions with atoms so they must be particles. Chadwick showed that the new particle had the predicted mass of 1, the same as the proton, and he called it the *neutron*.

The main details of the atom and its nucleus were now complete. Every atom

Two great Cambridge scientists of the early 1900s, Ernest Rutherford (right) and Joseph John Thomson (left). At the Cavendish laboratory both investigated the structure of atoms and the theory of electricity. Thomson was awarded the Nobel prize for physics in 1906; Rutherford the 1908 prize for chemistry. Rutherford developed the theory of the atom as a nucleus surrounded by electrons. His notes on his 'theory of structure of atoms' survive.

has a nucleus containing a certain number of protons, surrounded by an equal number of orbiting electrons. And where the mass of the atom is greater than that expected from the number of protons in its nucleus (which it is for all elements except hydrogen), the additional mass is supplied by neutrons. The nuclei of isotopes have the same number of protons but differ in the number of neutrons.

Consider again our previous examples, set out above in Table 1. The table shows that the element hydrogen has one electron orbiting round one proton, giving a total mass of 1. Carbon has six electrons orbiting round a nucleus containing six protons and six neutrons, giving a total mass of 12. The two isotopes of neon have the same number of protons and electrons, but one contains two extra neutrons.

Element	A	B	C	D	E
Hydrogen	1	1	0	1	1·00
Carbon	6	6	6	12	12·00
Neon 20	10	10	10	20	20·18
Neon 22	10	10	12	22	
(Ionium)	90	90	140	230	232·1
Thorium	90	90	142	232	

Table 1. Key: **A** No. of electrons. **B** No. of protons in nucleus. **C** No. of neutrons in nucleus. **D** Mass. **E** Atomic weight.

Naturally occurring neon and thorium consist of mixtures of several isotopes.

Equipped with this picture of the atom and its structure, chemists can explain most of the common properties and reactions of the elements.

Atoms by weight and number

The atomic nucleus is surrounded by a whirling mass of electrons whose erratic orbits can never be plotted. Yet their configurations determine the chemical identity of all matter.

FOR 2,000 YEARS, ever since the time of the Ancient Greeks, scientists held the belief that everything in the world is made from four fundamental elements – air, earth, fire and water. However, as seventeenth- and eighteenth-century experimentalists began renouncing armchair speculations in favour of stubborn laboratory facts, it became evident that air, earth, fire and water are neither fundamental nor are they elements.

The loss of this cherished belief, while a shattering blow in itself, soon palled before the realization that there was nothing to replace it. Instead of just four universal building blocks, there were now eight, ten, twelve, twenty, fifty. By the 1860s, the total number of known elements had passed three score, and there was no end in sight. Today there are 103. How were the chemists ever to make sense out of their burgeoning accumulation of re- actions and compounds if each element differed from every other element, and if new elements were being discovered all the time?

Fortunately, just about the time the problem seemed to be getting out of hand, a partial solution appeared on the horizon in the form of an amazing classification scheme proposed by the Russian chemist Dmitri Mendeleef in 1869. Not only was Mendeleef able to show definite kinship relations between elements which appar- ently had little in common, he was even able to predict the existence of certain elements long before they were actually discovered. From the vantage point of twentieth-century knowledge, we now believe we know how Mendeleef's re- markable periodic table is able to do the things that it does.

Numbers for atoms

The chemical properties of an element are determined by the number of its electrons or protons. This quantity is called the *atomic number*. The combined masses of the protons and neutrons in the nucleus is called the *mass number*. Some elements exist in several forms called isotopes. All the isotopes of a single element have the same number of protons (and electrons) but differ in their numbers of neutrons. So the isotopes of an element have the same atomic number but different mass num- bers. It is the atomic number which gives an element its separate identity; two atoms of different mass numbers may both be the same element, but two atoms with different atomic numbers – that is, differ- ent numbers of protons – can never be the same.

The *atomic weight* is the weight of an element as it occurs in nature relative to the weight of carbon, arbitrarily fixed at

12·00 as a standard. If an element has more than one naturally occurring isotope, then the atomic weight is the average weight of the isotopes calculated with consideration given to their relative proportions. For this reason, the atomic weight of an element is seldom a whole number and seldom the same as the mass number.

One isotope of lithium has 3 protons and 3 neutrons in its nucleus, giving a mass number of 6. But the atomic weight of lithium is 6·940 because of a significant contribution by an isotope with 3 protons and 4 neutrons; that is, mass number of 7. The average of these two isotopes is 6·940 rather than exactly 6·500 because there is much more naturally occurring lithium 7 than there is lithium 6.

According to Niels Bohr's original theory enunciated in 1913, the electrons of an atom occupy circular or elliptical orbits round the nucleus, something like the planets of the solar system going round the sun. The electrons described by the more sophisticated quantum theory are not quite so well-behaved. Though they tend to remain at predictable distances from the nucleus, they also tend to fly in all directions, rather than following a well-defined orbit. The result is a three-dimensional cloud, or shell, effect instead of the circles or ellipses.

Each one of these clouds, or shells, is given a particular quantum number and is further differentiated into various energy levels, or sub-groups, identified by appropriate letters. Each energy level in turn corresponds to a certain number of *orbitals,* each of which can hold a maximum of two electrons. So the number of electrons each shell can accommodate is limited by the number of orbitals in each sub-group. An *s* energy level corresponds to only 1 orbital and thus can hold only 2 electrons, a *p* energy level corresponds to 3 orbitals and can hold up to 6 electrons, a *d* energy level can hold 10 electrons, and an *f*

Above, Dmitri Mendeleef, a foremost pioneer of modern chemistry. Through his detailed labour on the system of classifying elements by their chemical properties he was able to prophesy the discovery of new elements to fill gaps in his table. One of the most recently made transuranium elements was named Mendelevium (Md 101). Evidence for the most up-to-date theories of atomic structure derives from experiments in huge accelerators which bombard atoms with high-speed sub-atomic particles. *Right,* an atom of a steel bar breaks up dramatically under the impact of a proton. Fragments of the broken atom fly off and are recorded on photographic emulsion (the darkest tracks are bits of nucleus).

22

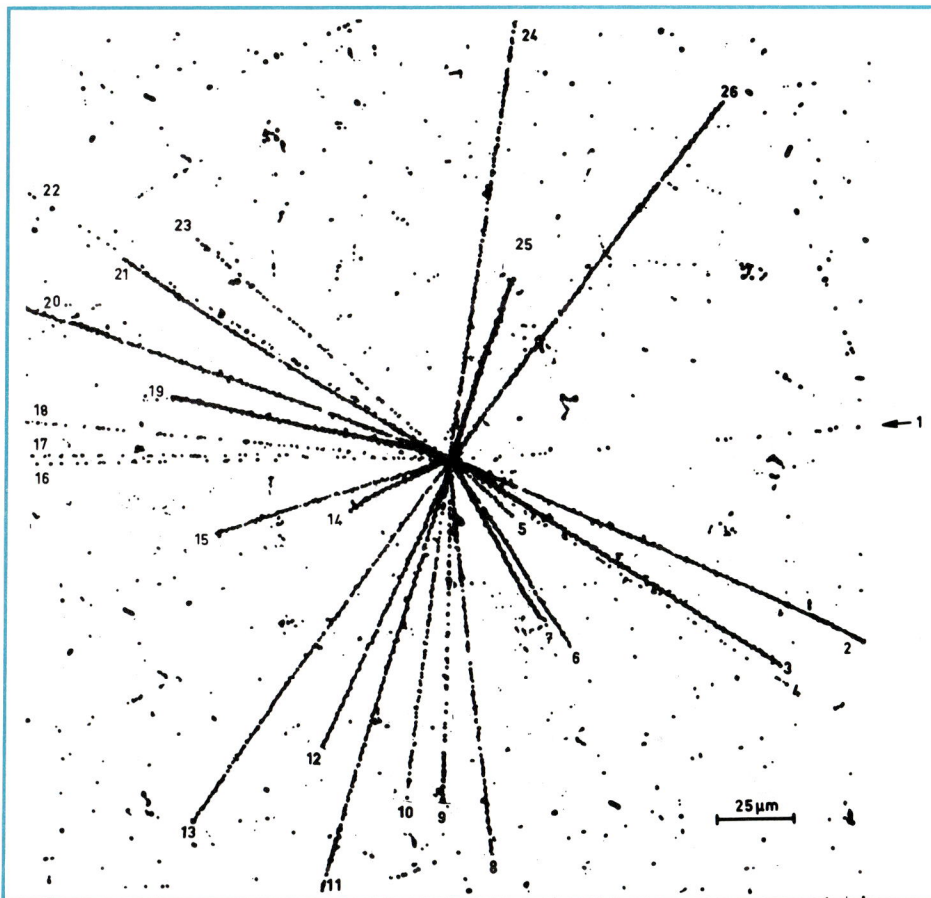

energy level can hold 14 electrons.

Tidy electron shells

From the point of view of elementary chemistry, it is only the outermost electron cloud or shell which is of much interest, because it is the outermost shell which largely determines what kinds of chemical reactions an element will take part in.

Consider a simple example. Hydrogen, which has the distinction of being the only element one of whose isotopes has no neutrons in the nucleus, has only 1 electron circling its nucleus. Since the first shell of an element can hold a maximum of 2 electrons, this first shell of hydrogen is only partially filled, quite an unsatisfactory situation. There are two possible solutions: either the hydrogen atom can pick up an electron from some other element in order to complete its first shell, or it can throw off its electron and so have a completely empty first shell. The latter is the more common.

By contrast, fluorine has a total of 9

electrons – 2 in a completed first shell and 7 in its second shell. However, the second shell is capable of holding 8 electrons. So fluorine has an incomplete shell just like hydrogen, but in this case there is no question as to what it is going to do about it. It is much easier to pick up the 1 electron needed to complete the shell than it is to throw off 7 to empty the shell.

The act of either picking up electrons or throwing them off in order to complete or empty a partially filled shell is the fundamental process of a simple chemical reaction. Under the proper conditions, then, hydrogen will gladly throw off its solitary electron to empty its first shell and fluorine will happily accept it in order to complete its second shell. The result of this swap is the gaseous compound hydrogen fluoride, HF. Since hydrogen has thrown off a negative electron, it now has a net positive electrical charge. Conversely, since fluorine has taken on an electron, it now has a net negative charge. So the two pieces of the compound, called ions, are held together by electrical attraction in an ionic bond.

If we look at an element such as oxygen, we find that it has 8 electrons – 2 in a completed first shell, and 6 in an incompleted second shell. Since the second shell can be satisfied with 8 electrons, oxygen gladly picks up 2 electrons whenever it can. If it is combining with hydrogen, it picks up one electron from each of two hydrogen atoms to give the familiar substance H_2O, or water. This process is slightly different from the formation of hydrogen fluoride, because the electrons are not actually transferred but shared. This is called co-valent bonding. Hydrogen fluoride shows some characteristics of this 'co-valent bonding', as well as simple ionic bonding in which the bonding electrons are quite separate.

The number of electrons an element is capable of accepting or giving away in a chemical reaction is called its valence

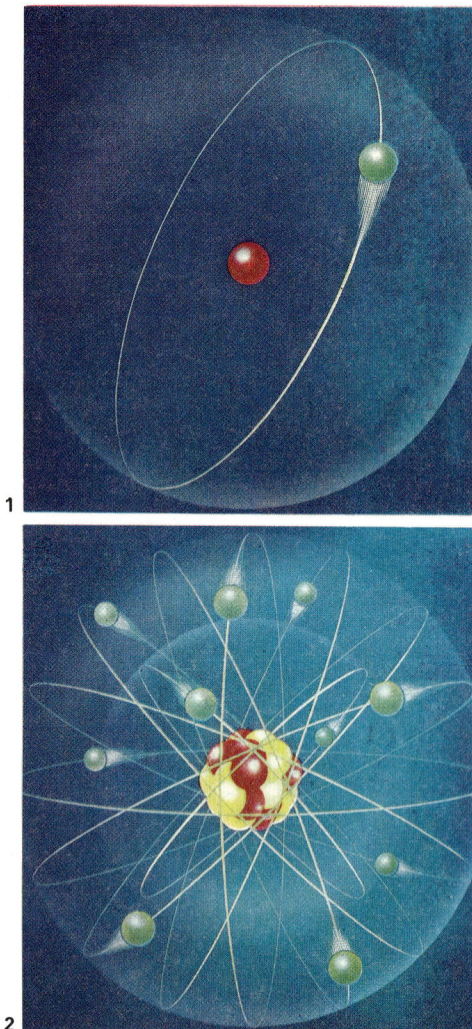

The building blocks of the atom – protons, neutrons and electrons – can be visualized so as to explain the properties of each element. **1** Hydrogen, simplest of the elements, has only one proton and one electron orbiting in the *s* subgroup of the first shell. Helium and lithium, **4**, the next two elements, are more complicated, having more particles. In helium, *left,* two orbiting electrons fill the first shell, so the

3

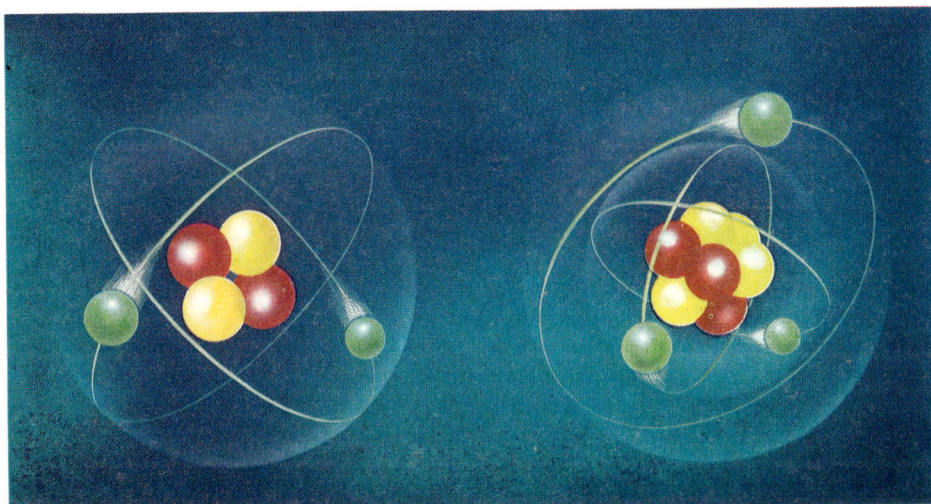

4

third electron which lithium possesses, *right*, has to orbit in the next shell, at a *2s* energy level. The nuclei of these atoms are made up of protons and neutrons; helium has two of each, but the lithium atom shown has three protons and four neutrons. This is an isotope of lithium known as lithium 7. Neon, **2,** is the first element to have a completely filled second shell with ten electrons orbiting in all the 1 and 2 energy sub-groups. *Co-valent* bonds between atoms form electrically stable compounds. Water, **3,** is formed in this way when two hydrogen atoms share electrons with a single oxygen atom in a tenacious atomic grip.

number. If the element gives electrons away, the valence number is prefixed with a positive sign (because the resulting ion is electrically positive) and if it accepts electrons its valence number is prefixed with a negative (because the resulting ion is electrically negative). Thus, the valence number of hydrogen would be $+1$, fluorine -1, and oxygen -2. Some elements have more than one valence number, because they can throw off or accept different numbers of electrons under different conditions.

Since the chemical properties of an element depend largely on the number of electrons in the outermost shell, we would expect to find striking similarities among all elements whose outermost shells hold the same number of valence electrons. To a great extent, this is correct, though it is not necessary to know anything about atomic structure in order to observe such a pattern.

As far back as 1864, the British industrial chemist John Newlands noticed that when he arranged the elements in order of increasing atomic weight, elements with similar properties were situated at every eighth position along the series. These groups of eight Newlands called *octaves*. About six years later, a German physicist named Julius Lothar Meyer studied the physical properties of the elements and also correlated them with atomic weights. When he plotted a graph of an atomic parameter, based on a physical property such as density or specific heat, against atomic weight, he obtained a graph shaped rather like a chain of mountain peaks with valleys between them. Elements on similar parts of the curves were found to have similar chemical properties.

At almost exactly the same time, Dmitri Mendeleef, a Russian chemist, published his now famous periodic table. He also arranged the elements in families, but left gaps where necessary to make elements with similar properties fall into vertical columns called groups.

Mendeleef made some remarkable predictions about the undiscovered elements to fill the gaps in his table. For example, he predicted the properties of a metallic element to fill the gap below aluminium and next to zinc. When gallium was discovered in 1875, it was found to confirm the almost uncanny accuracy of Mendeleeff's predictions. The 'missing' element below silicon in group IV was called 'eka-silicon' by Mendeleeff. He predicted it would be a greyish-white unreactive metal and have an atomic weight of about 73.

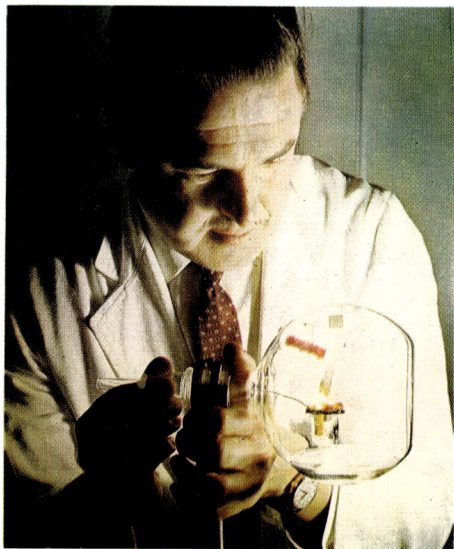

For centuries Man has tried to understand and control chemical reactions, what was once largely a process of trial and error can now be predicted and explained by modern theories of atomic structure and interrelationships.

The missing element

Fifteen years later, the German chemist Clemens Winkler discovered an element called germanium. It turned out to be a greyish-white metal which does not dissolve in acids or alkalis and which has an atomic weight of 72·60. Germanium was the missing 'eka-silicon'.

The modern versions of the table (there are several) substantially differ from the original offered by Mendeleef in 1869; however, the main features remain the same (see diagram, p. 29). The most obvious feature of the table is its arrangement into numbered columns and rows, plus the huge block without numbers, called transition elements, and the Lanthanide Series (called the 'rare earth' elements) and the Actinide Series. The transition elements and the rare earth elements represent an apparent disruption of our nice, orderly arrangement and will be dealt with in due course. The whole number under each element is its atomic number.

Each column, called a group, brings together those elements which have the same number of electrons in their outermost shell, i.e. they have the same valence. (The letter following each group number is a refinement which need not concern us, and will be omitted in what follows.) For example, hydrogen (H) in group I has only 1 electron, that in the first shell. Directly below it is lithium (Li), with 2 electrons in a completed first shell and 1 in an incompleted second shell. Sodium (Na) has 2 electrons in a completed first shell, 8 electrons in its completed second shell, and 1 electron in its third. And so on down the line. Each succeeding element in the group also has only one electron in its outermost shell. At first glance they may not resemble each other too closely (hydrogen is a gas, sodium is a soft solid), but because they each have a solitary electron in the outermost shell, and consequently the same valence, they enter into similar chemical reactions. Because of special properties of lithium and the elements directly below lithium in the table, they are collectively called alkali metals.

The same thing applies to group II. Each element has 2 electrons in its outermost shell; and thus, despite marked physical differences, they all undergo similar chemical reactions. Likewise with groups III–VIII, also labelled with an 'O'.

Arranging the elements

If we look across the periodic table from left to right, we see the elements arranged into rows called periods. The original reason for arranging the elements in this way was so that each succeeding element as one travels from left to right would have a higher atomic weight. This is important, because it led Mendeleeff to suspect that some of the atomic weights that had been calculated in his day were wrong. They just did not go into the table where he thought they should. In several instances, he was correct. These elements, with their revised atomic weights, now fit quite nicely where Mendeleef said they should.

However, a few elements still refused to co-operate, such as tellurium (Te) and iodine (I). In period 5 near the right-hand side, iodine follows tellurium, but has an atomic weight of 126·92, while tellurium has an atomic weight of 127·61. Such discrepancies were quite a nettlesome problem to the early researchers, but today we can explain them quite easily in terms of isotopes, which were not known to exist in Mendeleef's time. Every element was thought to have one form and one form only. Thus, the periods are no longer arranged in terms of ascending atomic weights, which are not completely regular, but ascending atomic numbers. Each succeeding element has in its nucleus one more proton (and perhaps several more neutrons) than its predecessor, and so the atomic numbers are continuous from 1 to 103.

Now, what about those awkward transition elements and rare earths which play so much havoc with our orderly arrangement? The fact is, they don't really play any havoc at all; they behave precisely as Nature dictates they must. It is we who play havoc with Nature's arrangement by insisting that all the elements should fit into a pattern of columns and rows.

To find out just what arrangement Nature intends, we must again look at electron configurations and employ a bit of quantum mechanics.

Twentieth-century research has shown that the first electron shell can hold a maximum of 2 electrons, the second shell a maximum of 8 electrons, the third shell a maximum of 18 electrons, and the fourth

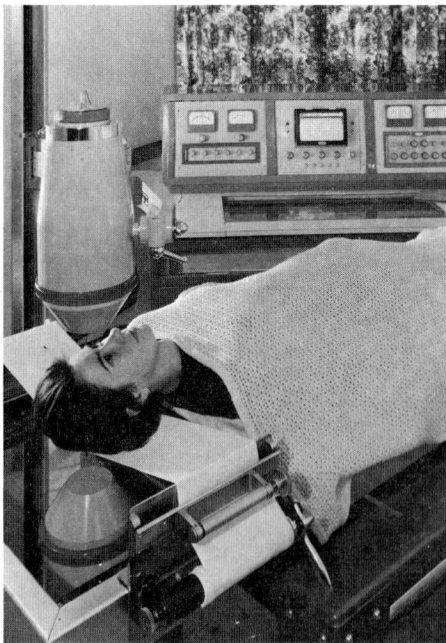

Radio-isotopes (unstable isotopes of ordinary elements made by artificially adding neutrons to nuclei in nuclear reactors or accelerators) give off characteristic radiation which can be easily detected by electronic instruments. *Above*, a brain scan records the variations in concentration of a radio-isotope administered to help detect abnormalities.

and higher shells a maximum of 32 electrons. However, one of the fundamental conclusions of quantum mechanics is that no *outermost* shell can ever hold more than 8 electrons. The elements of group 'O' are known as the 'inert gases' and confirm this conclusion, because they enter into nearly no chemical combinations at all. They have 8 electrons in their outermost orbits and are quite satisfied with the situation.

Shells within shells

The first element with a potential of having more than 8 electrons in the outermost shell is potassium, with an atomic number of 19. Its first shell is completely filled with 2 electrons, its second shell is completely filled with 8 electrons, leaving only 9 electrons for the third shell, which we know can take up to 18. However, this third shell is the outermost shell, and from quantum mechanics we know that the outermost shell can never have more than 8 electrons in it. So the ninth electron begins a fourth shell. More succinctly, instead of the electron configuration 2, 8, 9 one might expect from non-quantum considerations, the actual configuration is 2, 8, 8, 1. Thus, potassium (K) has a lone electron in its outermost shell and is a member of group I.

Calcium, with an atomic number of 20, follows a similar pattern. Instead of the expected configuration of 2, 8, 10, two electrons from the third shell are shifted into the fourth, giving a configuration of 2, 8, 8, 2. So calcium has a pair of valence electrons and consequently falls into group II.

With the examples of potassium and calcium to guide us, we might expect the next element, scandium, to arrange its 21 electrons in a pattern 2, 8, 8, 3. This is another case of Man trying to impose an order on Nature which Nature never intended. The actual electron configuration is 2, 8, 9, 2. Again, quantum mechanics explain why this happens, but even without delving into complex mathematics, we should not be too surprised that it does. After all, the third shell is quite capable of holding up to 18 electrons, providing that it is not the outermost shell. With 2 electrons now in the fourth shell, the third shell is no longer the outermost and thus is quite ready to take on its full complement of electrons.

Each succeeding element after scandium adds at least one more electron to the third shell. (Chromium and copper add 2 by reclaiming 1 electron from the third shell, giving them configurations of 2, 8, 13, 1 and 2, 8, 18, 1 respectively.) It is only after the third shell finally has been completed that more electrons begin occupying the fourth

shell again. So every element from scandium to zinc, with the exception of chromium and copper, has only two electrons in its outermost shell, and thus must belong to group II. Gallium, with an electronic configuration of 2, 8, 18, 3, finally gives us a new member of group III. Thus, all the elements from scandium to zinc may be thought of as a kind of bridge between group II and group III. This is one reason why they are called transition elements.

The fourth shell is now the outermost shell, and so must conform to the 'Rule of Eight'. Just as one would expect, when the fourth shell has acquired 8 electrons, a fifth shell is started. This happens with the element rubidium, which has an elec-

IA	IIA	IIIA	IVA	VA	VIA	VIIA	VIII			IB	IIB	IIIB	IVB	VB	VIB	VIIB	O
H 1																	He 2
Li 3	Be 4											B 5	C 6	N 7	O 8	F 9	Ne 10
Na 11	Mg 12											Al 13	Si 14	P 15	S 16	Cl 17	Ar 18
K 19	Ca 20	Sc 21	Ti 22	V 23	Cr 24	Mn 25	Fe 26	Co 27	Ni 28	Cu 29	Zn 30	Ga 31	Ge 32	As 33	Se 34	Br 35	Kr 36
Rb 37	Sr 38	Y 39	Zr 40	Nb 41	Mo 42	Tc 43	Ru 44	Rh 45	Pd 46	Ag 47	Cd 48	In 49	Sn 50	Sb 51	Te 52	I 53	Xe 54
Cs 55	Ba 56	✳ 57-71	Hf 72	Ta 73	W 74	Re 75	Os 76	Ir 77	Pt 78	Au 79	Hg 80	Tl 81	Pb 82	Bi 83	Po 84	At 85	Rn 86
Fr 87	Ra 88	★ 89·															

Lanthanides

✳	La 57	Ce 58	Pr 59	Nd 60	Pm 61	Sm 62	Eu 63	Gd 64	Tb 65	Dy 66	Ho 67	Er 68	Tm 69	Yb 70	Lu 71

Actinides

★	Ac 89	Th 90	Pa 91	U 92	Np 93	Pu 94	Am 95	Cm 96	Bk 97	Cf 98	Es 99	Fm 100	Mv 101	No 102	Lw 103

Table of the elements arranged to show resemblances. Solid blue indicates those elements built up by the regular addition of protons, neutrons and electrons on the appropriate energy levels. Further down the table the addition of electrons becomes much less regular, and lower energy levels are not always the first to be filled.

tronic configuration of 2, 8, 18, 8, 1, and so is a member of group I. The next element, strontium, also adds an electron to the fifth shell (2, 8, 18, 8, 2), and thus is a member of group II. But the next element, yttrium, in a manner very similar to that of scandium, adds a ninth electron to the fourth shell instead of a third electron to the fifth, giving the configuration 2, 8, 18, 9, 2. And so we have the beginning of another series of transition elements running from yttrium to cadmium.

'Rare earths'

Two more series of transition elements appear in the fifth and sixth periods. These series are often separated from the main body of the periodic table and grouped together under the name 'rare earths'.

The development of the periodic table and all the theory necessary to explain it has greatly enhancèd the chemist's understanding of what happens in his test-tubes, and thus has given him greater control over what happens in his test-tubes. Though a bit arduous at first, all of this theoretical interpretation of chemical reactions is directly responsible for most of the plastics, synthetic vitamins, patent medicines, man-made fibres and other benefits of the chemical laboratory. It has even allowed for the creation of new elements which never existed until Man called them into being.

The family life of electro-magnetic waves

Ordinary light and exotic X-rays are kith and kin in the family of electro-magnetic waves. The study and application of electro-magnetic waves has significantly altered everyday life.

WHEN IN 1690 Christiaan Huygens first put forward the idea that light is not particle-like in nature but travels in the form of waves, he could hardly have foreseen how far-reaching his theory would be. Of course he had no means of telling whether or not there were other forms of waves having similar properties to light. But we now know that light waves are just a small part of a whole family of radiant energy called electro-magnetic waves, which range from radio waves to X-rays and gamma rays. Light is the part of the spectrum we can see. Other parts, such as infra-red, ultra-violet, X-rays, and gamma rays, can be 'seen' by photographic plates. Radio waves can be detected using an aerial and suitable amplifying equipment.

Sir Isaac Newton and other early investigators had shown that white light can be split up by a prism into a range of colours from red to violet which form the visible spectrum. Later, the wave properties of each colour – its speed, wavelength, and frequency – were examined. It was found that in a given medium, such as air, the speed of each colour was the same (nearly 30 thousand million centimetres per second). But their frequencies and wavelengths differ, ranging from about 0·00004 cm and 750 billion cycles per second for violet light to 0·000075 cm and 400 billion cycles per second for red light.

Heat and colour

In 1800, Sir William Herschel investigated the amount of heat associated with each colour in the spectrum. He detected more heat at the red end of the visible spectrum than at the violet end, and surprisingly he measured even more heat at a position past the visible end of the spectrum beyond the red. He had discovered the first invisible light-like waves, now known as infra-red radiation. It was soon realized that heat waves occupy a region in the electro-magnetic spectrum next to light waves.

As their name suggests, electro-magnetic waves can also be produced electrically (over a certain range). An electric current flowing in a wire produces electric and magnetic fields around the wire. If the current alternates (a.c.), so do the fields.

When the frequency of the alternating current is small, the magnetic field around a wire carrying it is very much stronger

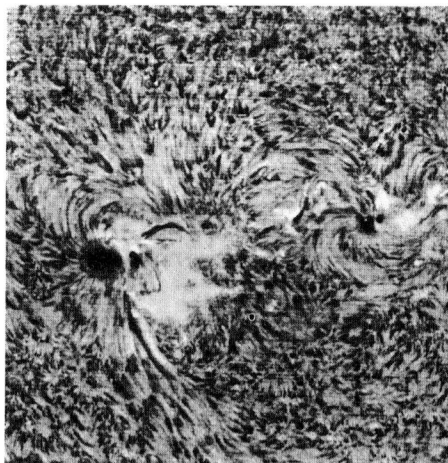

The fundamental research of the German Heinrich Hertz, *above left,* established basic properties of the electro-magnetic spectrum and led to modern radio communications. Spectroheliographs of the sun show vast pulsating hydrogen clouds surrounding sunspots, *right.* Such pictures are made by recording only hydrogen-associated wavelengths. Absorption spectra of thallium, *bottom,* show identifiable characteristic lines.

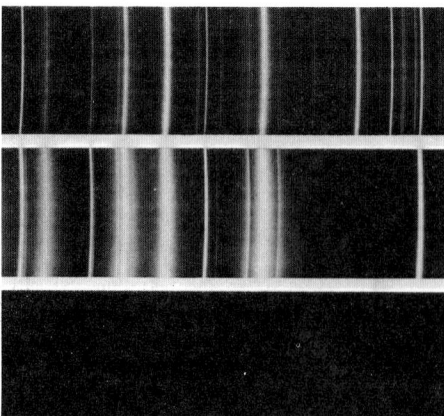

than is the electric field, and no significant electro-magnetic wave is produced. As the frequency of the current increases, the electric field increases until, at frequencies of 10 to 15 kilocycles per second, an electro-magnetic wave is radiated, having the same frequency as the frequency of the alternating current in the wire. These forms of waves were first investigated by the German physicist Heinrich Hertz (1857–94) and were known as Hertzian waves; we now call them radio waves.

As a belated recognition of the pioneering work done by Hertz, in 1966 radio stations around the world began giving their frequencies in 'kilohertz' or 'megahertz' instead of the standard 'kilocycle' or 'megacycles'. There is, of course, no difference between a 'hertz' and a 'cycle'. A frequency of 200 kilohertz and 200 kilocycles are exactly the same.

Using radio wavelengths of 150 metres (frequencies of 2 megacycles per second) and less, it is possible to communicate across the Atlantic Ocean. This is because the radio waves zig-zag around the Earth by bouncing backwards and forwards between the surface and ionized layers in the upper atmosphere (called the ionosphere). The ionosphere can act as a kind of mirror to radio waves down to about 7 or 8 metres wavelength. Shorter wavelengths, such as those used for VHF (very high frequency) radio and television, pass through it. Radio waves originating from distant stars and galaxies also have short wavelengths; they penetrate the ionosphere and can be received at the Earth's surface. These very short wavelengths are used for radar and for communicating with orbiting satellites and space vehicles.

Hertz showed the physical similarity between radio waves and light waves. At high frequencies, about 1,500 megacycles per second and above, micro-waves, the electro-magnetic radio waves, behave in many respects as do light waves. For this reason, micro-wave aerials are constructed on similar basic principles as are reflecting light telescopes, with large reflecting concave 'bowls' to 'focus' the waves. Radio telescopes such as that at Jodrell Bank in Cheshire, are used to 'listen' to radio waves from distant stars. Satellite communications aerials such as that at Goonhilly also use these principles.

Another property of micro-waves is that they can be passed along closed pipes called *waveguides*. The radio wave can be thought of as bouncing down the waveguide. This is the way in which micro-wave signals are conducted in radar sets and communications equipment.

Cooking by micro-wave

At very short wavelengths, micro-waves exhibit some of the properties of infra-red radiation, their near neighbours in the electro-magnetic spectrum. For example, they produce heat when passed through a substance and are used in micro-wave 'cookers' for food. The micro-waves pass right through the food and heat it all over at once, unlike the situation in a conventional cooker which heats the food from the outside surfaces only. For this reason, micro-wave cooking is extremely rapid.

The shorter wavelength infra-red region of the electro-magnetic spectrum was known 150 years ago, but the existence of longer wavelength infra-red waves was not proved until sometime later. During the early part of this century, experiments into the reflecting and refracting properties of certain crystals revealed the existence of infra-red wavelengths of up to a tenth of a millimetre. Since the upper wavelength limit of micro-waves is also in this range, the continuity of the electro-magnetic spectrum at this point was established.

Infra-red waves are given out by all hot

A micro-wave oven, **1**, can heat food better and faster than standard models, because it is able to heat it right through. Dropping low on the horizon, the setting sun appears gloriously red as the intervening air scatters most other colours away from our eyes, **2**. The blue of the sky is also caused by scattering.

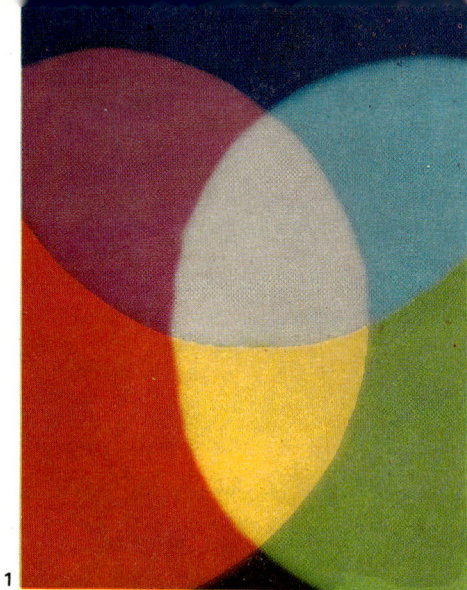

an aircraft's jet engines. But perhaps the most important infra-red radiation to Man is the heat waves arriving on Earth from the sun.

The continuity of the electro-magnetic spectrum from infra-red to visible light was known early in the days of the wave theory. We can demonstrate this continuity by heating an object such as a metal bar. At first the metal becomes hot without glowing, and we can feel the heat coming from it in the form of infra-red waves. As more heat is supplied to the bar, it begins to glow a dull red (corresponding to longest wavelength light waves), gradually changes to a yellowish colour (shorter wavelength), before glowing white hot when many infra-red and visible wavelengths are emitted together.

The visible spectrum is familiar to most people as a rainbow produced by the diffraction of light by small droplets of water in the air. When mixed together, the colours we see make up white light. We can also observe parts of the spectrum as the atomic spectra produced by individual elements, such as in sodium (yellow) and neon (orange) lighting. We can also produce any colour of light by simply using a source of white light masked by the appropriate colour filter, which allows only

1 With the exception of the three primary colours - red, green and blue - all other shades are mixtures, including white. Red and blue are also primary *paint* colours, but green is then a mixture of yellow and blue. When hot enough, even dull metal becomes incandescent and gives off light, the colour of which gives a clue to the temperature, **2** Different types of electro-magnetic waves are transmitted in different ways, depending on their properties. Long and medium waves may be bounced off satellites. Micro-waves are transmitted through underground pipes or waveguides, **3** Giant radio telescopes, **4** are used to detect radio signals emanating from outer space.

bodies, even those that are not sufficiently hot to produce visible light waves as well. In fact, black surfaces are the most efficient radiators of infra-red waves. Photographs may be taken using infra-red 'light' and suitable films, and infra-red viewing devices are used to 'see' at night when there is no illumination from visible light. Infra-red sights may be fitted to guns and rifles, and infra-red detectors often form the basis of the guidance system in ground-to-air and air-to-air missiles which seek out the hot gases from the exhaust of

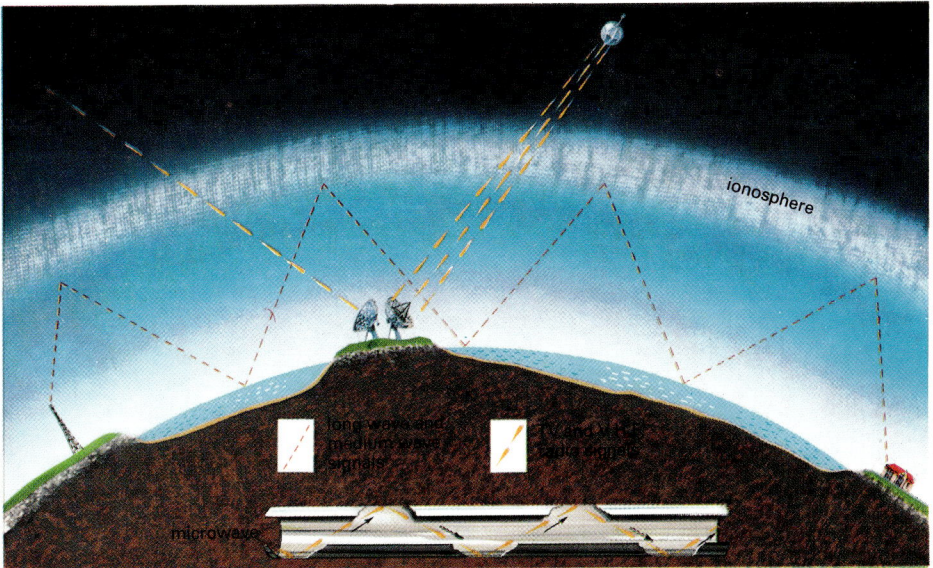

3

long-wave and
medium-wave
signals

microwave

ionosphere

4

waves of certain wavelengths to pass through.

Infra-red and visible light wavelengths can be measured using the important wave property of diffraction. By projecting the waves on to a specially-made diffraction 'grating', a pattern of light and dark bands is produced. From the arrangement and spacing of the bands, the wavelength of the radiation can be found.

Why a sunset is red

Light waves are easily scattered by small particles such as dust, and the amount of scattering depends on the wavelength of the light. Long wavelengths (red light) are scattered very little, but short wavelengths (blue) are easily scattered. We can observe this effect on a cloudless day when the sun sets. The sun and surrounding sky are red, because all the blue from the sun's white light has been scattered away by the dust particles in the atmosphere. The eastern sky, opposite the sunset, is blue because all we see is blue light scattered back from the dust; the red light passes out into space and is not scattered backwards at all. Infra-red photographs are unaffected by mist and haze because infra-red is not scattered by particles in the air.

Immediately next to the blue end of the visible spectrum is the ultra-violet region of the electro-magnetic spectrum. The sun emits ultra-violet waves (as well as infra-red and light waves), so the existence of ultra-violet was also established relatively early. We now know that ultra-violet light is important to animal physiology because it plays a part in the formation of vitamin D in the body – and it causes sun tan. People such as miners who spend much of their time away from the sun may need ultra-violet lamp treatment to replace the natural sunlight they miss. Ultra-violet waves can also be detected photographically, as can visible light and infra-red. But ultra-violet has different penetrating properties and will not pass through ordinary

glass. Materials such as nylon are transparent to ultra-violet, which will also pass through a thin foil of silver. Under ultra-violet 'light', white clothing washed in so-called 'whiter-than-white' detergents, which contain special additives, gives off visible light. This property gives the whitening effect to clothes when viewed in sunlight – they really are brighter! Ultra-violet wavelengths may be as short as a ten-millionth of a centimetre.

The discovery of X-rays

The electro-magnetic waves which lie beyond the ultra-violet were first investigated nearly 70 years ago by another German physicist, Wilhelm Konrad Röntgen (1845–1923). Röntgen was experimenting with high voltages applied across metal plates in a tube containing gas at low pressure. He called the new waves *X-rays*, and found that they had strong penetrating properties and also that they fogged photographic plates. (It was their effect on some of his stored plates near the experimental tube that first caused Röntgen to investigate the new waves.) It was later found that X-rays are emitted whenever a high-speed stream of electrons strikes a metal target enclosed in a tube similar to Röntgen's. When produced this way, X-rays span a broad spectrum as does visible light. Some X-rays also have certain special wavelengths, which can be compared to the single-wavelength light produced, for example, by sodium light. The special or *characteristic* X-ray wavelengths depend on the material from which the target in the tube is made. X-rays of extremely short wavelength, called gamma rays, are emitted by certain radioactive substances such as radium.

Following Huygens's theory on the wave properties of light, which in the opinion of most scientists satisfactorily explained diffraction, refraction and interference, the corpuscle versus wave battle died down. But when the photoelectric

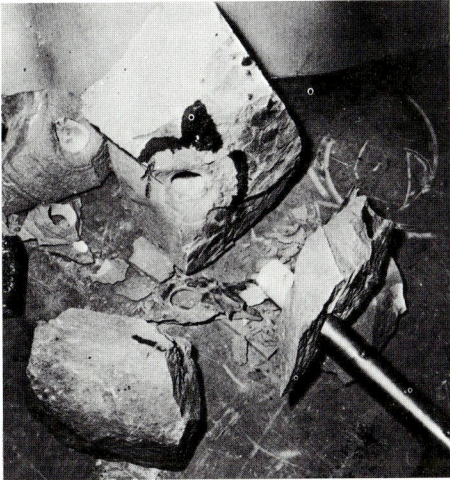

Modern radar equipment, *top left,* makes airline flights both smoother and safer. A panel of mirrors, *top right,* gathers in infra-red rays from the sun to heat water in this French solar energy central-heating system. A British 'ray gun', *below left,* splits rocks by using micro- wave energy to boil moisture content, causing violent expansion. This apparatus may some- day have important applications in quarrying and tunnelling, and even replace the noisy pneu- matic drill. An advanced radar, *below right,* spots aircraft as far away as France and Holland.

effect was discovered and investigated, the wave theory could not explain it and the long-forgotten particle or corpuscular theory, championed by Newton, seemed to fit. Max Planck then proposed, initially in connection with heat carried by electro-magnetic waves, that radiant energy can exist only as multiples of certain fixed quantities of energy, called quanta. According to the quantum theory, the energy of each quantum increases with increasing frequency.

This theory was then extended by Albert Einstein, who proposed that light radiation is composed of short bursts of waves, each burst or *photon* being a quantum of energy. In this way, the quantum theory effectively combines the corpuscular and wave theories and provides a convenient explanation of the photoelectric effect without abandoning the wave theory's convincing explanation of diffraction and so on. The quantum theory also explains why, say, sodium emits yellow light, and accounts for characteristic X-ray wavelengths in terms of electron 'jumps' between orbitals of different energies, which result in the emission or absorption of quanta of radiant energy. In the late 1920s G. P. Thomson showed which X-rays are diffracted by a crystal.

The wavelengths concerned are found to depend on the velocity of the electrons, and are in the range 1·0 to 0·1 Ångstrom units. (A hundred million Ångstrom units equal one centimetre.)

Seeing without light

Use is made of this property in the electron microscope; instead of using light, the microscope uses a beam of electrons 'fired' into the object to be studied. The power of any microscope to form a separate image of two close objects depends on the wavelength of the waves used. An electron microscope (using an electron 'wavelength' of 1 Ångstrom unit) is far more powerful than an optical microscope (using light wavelengths of about 5,000 Ångstrom units), and can resolve down to almost the size of a single atom.

In 1932, experiments showed that beams of atoms or molecules are also diffracted by crystals and exhibit wave properties. This was experimental proof that matter may behave either as particles or waves, the nature of the experiment determining which of these two facets is the more prominent. The new science of wave mechanics could now confidently be applied to the study of atoms and molecules.

Max Planck and the quantum

Waves which are particles, particles which are waves, and a form of mathematics which makes sense out of the paradox - this is the story of a startling revolution in twentieth-century physics.

THE STORY of the quantum theory spans the first 30 years of this century. It evolved as a result of scientists' attempts to explain theoretically certain physical phenomena, most of them concerned with radiant energy such as light and heat. At about the same time, other scientists were trying to learn more about the composition of the atom. Their theories were based on experimental studies of the properties of materials also involving radiation and radioactivity.

As more and more information emerged from the concerted efforts in these two fields of study, it became evident that the explanation of the properties of atoms and the particles of which they are composed and the explanation of the properties of radiant energy were not entirely dissimilar. It was found that one all-embracing theory could account for most of the observed facts; matter, particles, waves and radiation were all related and interconnected by the quantum theory and the branch of mathematics developed to handle it, called wave mechanics.

The impetus to theories on atomic structure – indeed the first real evidence that the atom *has* a structure ('atom' derives from Greek, meaning 'indivisible') – came with J. J. Thomson's discovery of the electron in 1897. Later, scientists dis-covered the proton and the neutron, and a picture of the way in which these particles are arranged within the atom began to emerge. The neutrons and protons were found to form the relatively massive central nucleus, and to be surrounded largely by empty space through which move the atom's electrons.

Then in 1913, Niels Bohr suggested that the electrons do not move about just anywhere, but are restricted to certain specific orbits. Different orbits correspond to electrons of different energy. From this description emerged the concept of energy 'levels' for electrons in the atoms of a material. This was the beginning of the idea that the energy distribution among the electrons in an atom is not continuous but is characterized by separate (*discrete*) energy levels. For an electron to change orbits, there has to be a change in its energy. For example, an electric field or heat can supply the necessary energy for an electron to move to an orbit of higher energy – that is, to move to a higher energy level.

Meanwhile, other workers were trying to understand what happens to the atoms of a material when it conducts electricity or gives off energy such as heat and light. They discovered that these phenomena were also concerned with the movement of

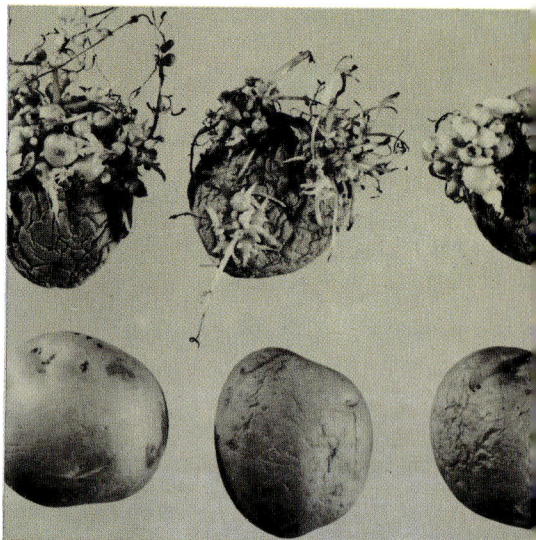

Nuclear radiation has an enormous potential for both good and evil. The tomato-plant stem covered with clusters of abnormal tumours, *left*, was exposed to 300 röntgens a day for several weeks. By contrast, the potatoes, *right*, were exposed to different amounts of radiation over a period of 16 months. One which received the largest dose remains firm and ready to eat. The other five show very noticeable deterioration.

electrons. When an electron changes orbits or 'falls' from one energy level to a level of lower energy, it emits the excess energy as radiation, which may take the form of X-rays, light or heat. It therefore follows that the energy emitted is not continuous, but composed of discrete levels just as is the energy absorbed by an atom.

Various unsuccessful attempts to explain the distribution of heat energy in a black body (a perfect radiator of heat) on the basis of 'classical' thermodynamics and electrodynamics were made by Wein and by Rayleigh and Jeans. Then in 1900, Max Planck (1858–1947) proposed his famous theory that all radiant energy – whether being absorbed by an atom or emitted by a black body – is composed of *quanta*. Each quantum of energy has a characteristic frequency given by the equation $E=h\nu$. where E is energy, ν is the frequency of the radiation concerned, and h is a constant called Planck's constant. Using this equation, Planck was able to account for the distribution of energy in a black body. The heat energy, formerly considered as continuous waves of radiation, was shown to consist of discrete quanta.

Where light strikes

Another phenomenon inexplicable by earlier wave theories of radiation is called the photoelectric effect. It occurs when light strikes certain metals to produce an electric current (as in the photocell of a photographer's light meter). In 1905, Albert Einstein (1879–1955) applied Planck's quantum theory to this problem and produced an entirely satisfactory explanation. Light energy is also composed of quanta, called *photons,* and when these strike the atoms of a metal they transfer enough of their energy to electrons to make them flow as an electric current.

A similar situation was discovered by A.H. Compton in 1923. Beams of X-rays are scattered by a slab of carbon, and their scattering is accompanied by a movement of electrons. This effect, called the Compton effect, is also explicable in terms of the quantum theory.

Heat quanta and photons are therefore 'packets' or particles of energy, and radiant energy is not continuous. A beam of light consists of millions of photons moving at a velocity of 186,000 miles a second. Experimenters were also studying beams of other known particles, particularly beams of electrons. The old name of 'cathode rays' has fallen into disuse, and a stream of millions of electrons produced by making a metal cathode *emit* at high voltages is called an electron beam. When the same particles are emitted from a radioactive substance, they are called beta-rays, but they also consist of electrons.

In 1927, two American physicists called Davisson and Germer succeeded in diffracting, or bending, beams of electrons by 'bouncing' them off metallic crystals. A year later, G.P. Thomson obtained diffraction patterns by passing an electron beam through a thin gold foil. Later workers produced diffraction patterns with atoms of hydrogen and helium. Now diffraction is one of the characteristic properties of wave motion, and in these experiments particles (electrons or atoms) were behaving as if they were waves. However, this behaviour is consistent with a hypothesis proposed by Louis de Broglie in 1924 – originally formulated to account for the Compton effect and the photoelectric effect – which states that all waves can be considered to consist of particles and that all particles can behave as if they are waves.

If electrons knocked out of atoms behave as if they were waves, why should not

The enunciation of the quantum theory around the turn of the century by Max Planck, *top*, created a revolution in scientific thought. Niels Bohr, *centre*, furthered acceptance of the theory when he applied it to his model of the structure of the hydrogen atom. However, persistent difficulties led to the belief that energy has both a wave and a particle nature. Erwin Schrödinger, *below*, fashioned this idea into wave mechanics.

Fundamental to research in atomic physics is the geiger counter, *above*, an instrument for measuring radioactive emissions. The counter shown in the photograph is being lowered into a nuclear fission training reactor in the U.S.A.

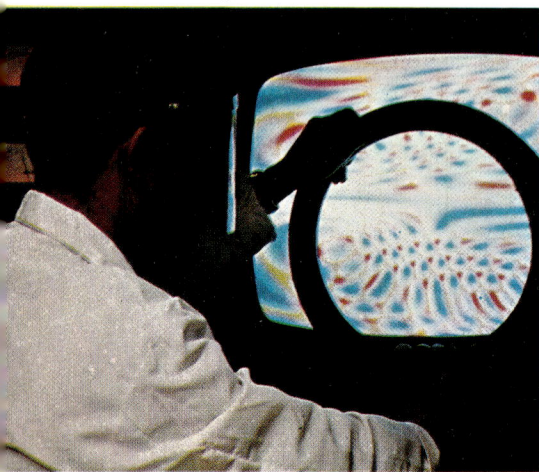

electrons *inside* an atom behave in a similar way? The answer to a question of this sort was supplied by E. Schrödinger in 1926 when he formulated his wave equation for the hydrogen atom. Schrödinger approached the problem mathematically and replaced Bohr's idea of electrons in orbits with an equation that describes only where an electron is *likely* to be in space in terms of its energy. The highly complex mathematics involved is called *wave mechanics*, in recognition of the dual wave-particle nature of the electron.

A British technician, *left*, demonstrates a practical application of fundamental research - colour television. The picture on the screen is produced by a stream of electrons fired from an electron gun inside. Nuclear fission and television are both the progeny of theoretical and practical research into the nature of matter carried out largely, but not entirely, in the twentieth century.

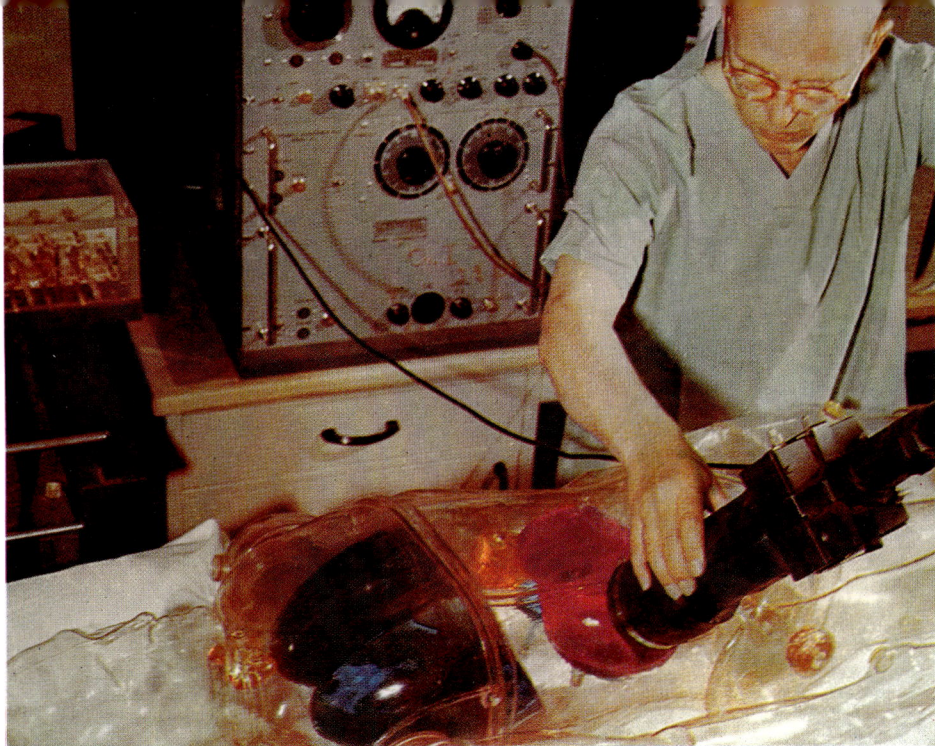

The mannequin, *above*, is not being prepared for burial. It has been exposed to atomic radiation and is being prepared for insertion into a type of machine which will measure absorption of radiation by the plastic-encased skeleton. Experiments such as this one are essential in readying Man to go into space and in evolving new medical techniques here on the Earth. The botanist, *left*, checks the results of a similar experiment carried out on snapdragons in order to detect genetic changes caused by radiation. Knowledge of how radiation affects plant growth could be a key weapon in the war against hunger.

An alternative name for the special mathematics involved is *quantum statistics*. This name gives an insight into the physical interpretation of Schrödinger's wave equation. Further physical evidence was provided in 1927 by the physicist Heisenberg who proposed his uncertainty principle. This states, in effect, that it is impossible to see an electron anyway (even given a sufficiently powerful microscope). For us to be able to 'see' anything, it has to be illuminated. Even if we could capture a stationary electron and put it under some sort of super-microscope, we would have to shine a light on it to see it. As soon as a photon (a particle of light similar in size to an electron) came along to illuminate our electron, it would collide with it and knock it out of the way. Heisenberg's principle states that there is always an uncertainty about simultaneously knowing the velocity and position of a particle: if we know how fast it is moving we do not know where it is, and vice versa.

A good guess

This situation can be coped with mathematically by considering not an electron in a given position or orbit, but by considering the *probability* that an electron will be in a given region in space at a given time. That is, even though we cannot say precisely where an electron is or how fast it is moving at any point in time, we can make a pretty good guess. This involves a form of statistical analysis and applied to atomic physics is called quantum statistics. The Schrödinger wave equation may be interpreted using these techniques, and its physical significance is that it gives the probability distribution of the electrons in an atom – that is, the likelihood that an electron will be in a given energy level. The actual parameter used to describe the position of an electron is the square of the probability as it appears in the wave equation. This is analogous to the situation in ordinary waves where the square of the amplitude of a wave is proportional to the intensity of the wave concerned.

To solve the wave equation for actual atoms requires even more specialized mathematical techniques. Interpreting the overall *macroscopic* effects, i.e. those which we can easily observe by conventional means, of *microscopic* particles is one of the functions of statistical mechanics. Three approaches are commonly used, each based on a different set of assumptions, and they are named after the men who developed them. They are called Bose-Einstein statistics, Fermi-Dirac statistics, and Maxwell-Boltzmann statistics and use special mathematical functions such as those associated with their inven-

tors Legendre, Bessel, Hermite and Laguerre.

Using these mathematical techniques, it is possible to derive theoretically many of the fundamental relationships of the quantum theory and of other aspects of physical sciences. For example, by applying Bose-Einstein statistics to solve the wave equation relating to electron jumps generating quanta of heat energy, it is possible to obtain exactly the same equation as that originally postulated by Planck for the energy distribution in black-body radiation.

The energy possessed by an electron in an atom is made up of various forms, such as vibrational energy, rotational energy and so on. An electron spins on its axis, vibrates, carries an electric charge, and has an associated magnetic field. According to the quantum theory, each of these forms of energy is quantized, and each is assigned a quantum number that characterizes it. The regions in space around the nucleus occupied by electrons are now called *orbitals* (not orbits as in the Bohr model), and there is a limit to the number of electrons that can be accommodated in each orbital. That is, there is a limit to the number of electrons with the same energy.

Explaining the conundrums

However, if one orbital contained two electrons of the same energy which also had the same spin and so on, the two electrons would be indistinguishable. They could have no separate identity. This problem was recognized in 1925 by W. Pauli, who solved it by proposing his *exclusion principle,* which states that no two electrons in an atom can have all their quantum numbers the same. For example, if one electron is spinning, say, clockwise on its axis (corresponding to a spin quantum number of $\frac{1}{2}$), the other electron must be spinning anti-clockwise (and have a spin quantum number of $-\frac{1}{2}$). Another way of interpreting Pauli's exclusion

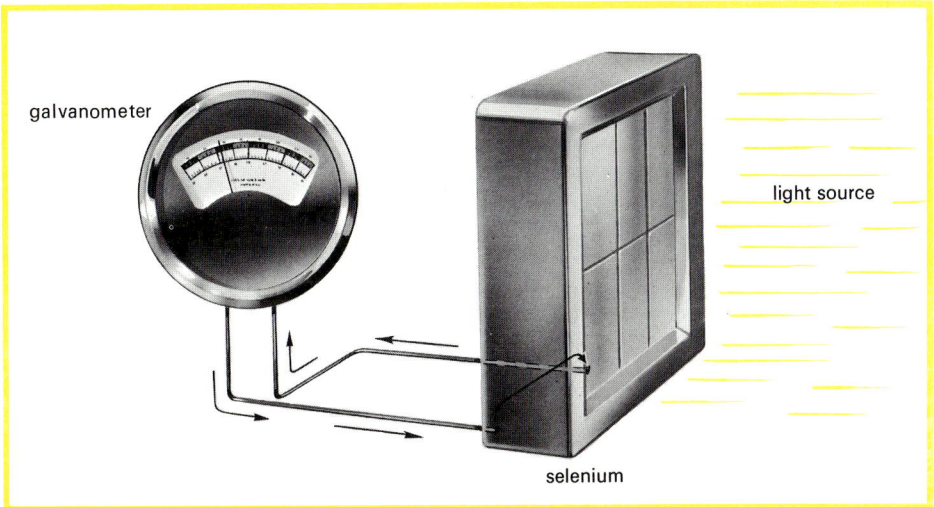

galvanometer

light source

selenium

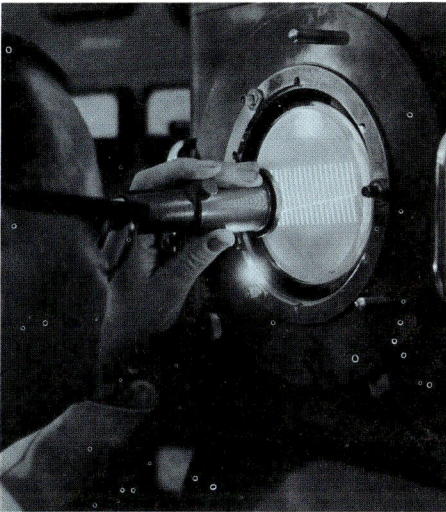

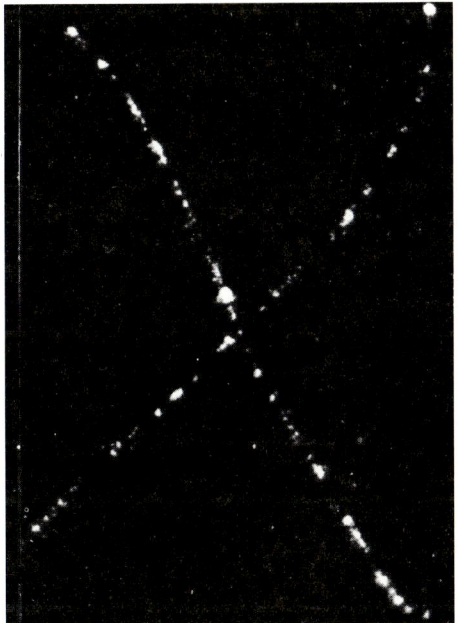

Light quanta, or photons, striking certain sensitive substances such as selenium can dislodge electrons, thus causing an electric current to flow. This is called the photoelectric effect, *top*, and this explanation based on quantum theory won Albert Einstein the 1921 Nobel Prize for physics. Other applications of the quantum theory are found in the cathode-ray tube, *below left*, and in the Wilson Cloud Chamber, *below right*, a device for studying atomic particles in flight.

45

The photograph of the leaf, *above*, was taken after it had absorbed some radioactive phosphorus, to study plant growth.

principle is to consider that it excludes the possibility that two electrons may both be at the same place at the same time.

Wolfgang Pauli was only 25 when, in 1925, he published the scientific paper setting out his exclusion principle. In 1945 he was awarded a Nobel Prize for this major achievement. By then he was one of the world's most noted physicists.

The development of quantum theory and wave mechanics has led to many interesting and useful applications. In the practical field, these two views of nature serve as the theoretical underpinning for research in preserving food by radiation, for treating cancer by radiation, for studying growth by radio-isotopes, and for protecting astronauts and cosmonauts from the hazards of space travel. Also, many conundrums of theoretical physics have given way under quantum and wave interpretations. The photoelectric effect is now understood, and new insights have been gained into the mysteries of chemical reactions and sub-atomic structures.

But perhaps the most unappreciated derivative of wave mechanics and quantum theory has been their influence on philosophy. Some prominent scientist-philosophers (scientists often take an interest in philosophy) have contended that the Heisenberg uncertainty principle re-establishes the Christian doctrine of free will, which came under such severe questioning in the wake of the theories of physics developed by Sir Isaac Newton and others in the seventeenth and early eighteenth centuries. Physical theories and laws which apparently predicted precisely future happenings led to a common acceptance of fatalism. Whether or not the philosophical interpretation of the uncertainty principle has any justification or will bear up under the test of time is yet to be determined, but the fact that science will continue to play an important role in influencing Man's view of himself stands without question.

Open secrets in an X-ray's beam

A mysteriously fogged photographic plate was among Wilhelm Röntgen's first clues to the strange rays loose in his laboratory. Today, art, science and medicine use the name he gave them.

MANY PEOPLE have at some time been X-rayed, either in hospital or at a mass X-ray unit. From X-ray pictures taken of a part of the body, doctors can detect and diagnose illness, examine bone structures, and even determine whether an unborn baby can be born naturally or requires a Caesarean birth.

But X-rays have many other important uses both in and out of medicine. For instance, hidden defects in metal structures can be detected by X-ray techniques, and the effects of crystal structures on X-rays is used to examine the forms of crystals and the arrangements of their atoms.

The discovery of X-rays in 1895 by the German physicist Wilhelm Röntgen was the result of investigations into quite different effects. Like many of his contemporaries, Röntgen was studying the newly observed cathode rays which were found to stream from the cathode of a low-pressure discharge tube when a high voltage was applied across its electrodes.

Cathode rays produce a bluish glow from the small amounts of gas or air left in the tube, and Röntgen had covered a tube with black paper to contain this light. He noticed, however, that a nearby zinc sulphide screen glowed or fluoresced when the voltage between the tube electrodes was about 10,000 volts. Also some of his photographic plates near the tube, although unexposed to light, became fogged during the experiments. Since both the tube and the plates were covered in black paper, light had certainly not caused this fogging. To trace the source of the effect, Röntgen set up near the tube a lead screen (he had found that this prevented the new 'rays' from passing) with four holes in it. Behind the screen he put a photographic plate, and then adjusted the tube to the correct conditions.

When the photographic plate was developed, it had four spots where rays passing through the holes in the lead screen had fallen on to it. By replacing the plate in its original position and tracing lines back from the spots through the holes in the screen, Röntgen showed that the new rays came from the end of the discharge tube where the cathode rays fell. Cathode rays, when given sufficient energy by a high electric potential across the tube, had caused certain rays to be given off on striking a 'target'. Röntgen called the new rays X-rays. Today, cathode rays are known to be a stream of electrons,

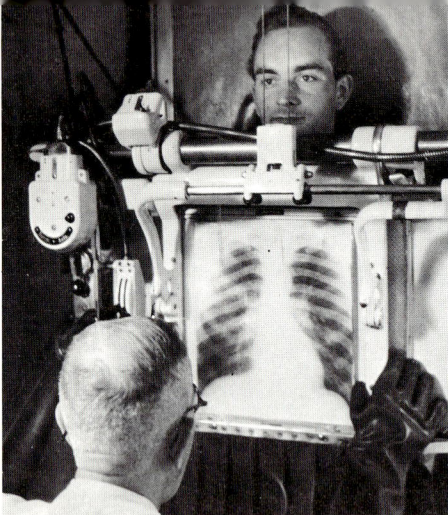

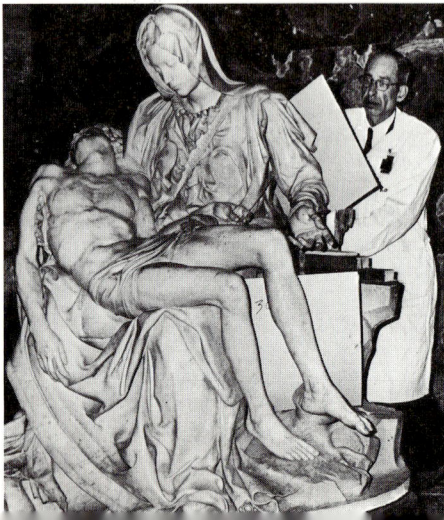

and, in general, any high-energy electron beam striking a metal target causes X-rays to be emitted.

Waves that could penetrate

X-rays were carefully studied to discover their nature. It was concluded that since they were unaffected by magnetic or electric fields (which a stream of charged particles such as electrons would be) and also travelled in straight lines, they must be similar in nature to light. By 1900, more evidence to support this idea had been found from diffraction patterns produced by X-rays. The form of the patterns suggested that if X-rays are waves like light, they have a much shorter wavelength. In 1912, the British physicist Sir William Henry Bragg succeeded in measuring the wavelengths of X-rays, using diffraction patterns produced by crystals, and, as expected, the wavelengths were very short. In this way, the relationship between light and X-rays was confirmed, and X-rays were recognized as a form of electromagnetic waves, as are visible light, radio and infra-red waves.

Early X-ray tubes used cathode rays in a similar way to Röntgen's discharge tube. But they were unreliable because the low pressure in the tube was difficult to maintain at a constant level and the quality of the X-rays was unpredictable. When techniques for maintaining low pressure improved, these early tubes were replaced by the Coolidge tube. In this, the stream of electrons previously provided by the cathode rays comes from a heated tungsten filament in rather the same way as in a thermionic valve or a television tube. The electrons are then 'fired' on to a metal target, the high voltage between the filament and the target giving the electrons sufficient energy to cause X-radiation as before.

The basic properties of X-rays were observed by Röntgen: their penetrating power, their ability to cause fluorescence, and their effect on photographic plates. Later wave properties were demonstrated, including diffraction, refraction, interference, an X-ray 'photoelectric' effect, and even polarization. This confirmed the kinship of X-rays and light.

Some of these properties of X-rays are used in the X-ray spectrometer, an important instrument developed by W. H. Bragg and his son W. L. (Sir Lawrence) Bragg to measure X-ray wavelengths accurately. It is basically similar to an optical spectrometer used for measuring light wavelengths. A narrow 'beam' of X-rays is directed at an acute angle on to a crystal mounted on a turntable. The crystal diffracts the X-rays in much the same way as a diffraction grating diffracts light, and the diffracted X-rays pass towards a detecting device. This consists of a tube filled with a gas such as methyl iodide, which absorbs X-rays strongly and which becomes ionized when X-rays pass through it. The electrical charge of the gas ions is then measured using an electrometer, giving an indication of the strength of the X-rays falling on to the tube. The energy associated with a particular wavelength can be studied by moving the crystal and the detecting device to the correct positions for that wavelength.

The wavelength itself is found by calculation, using a knowledge of the crystal structure (its dimensions, atomic weight, and so on) and the angles of alignment between the crystal and the detecting device. The relationship giving the wavelength is called Bragg's Law. For this work the Braggs were awarded a Nobel prize in 1915, when W. L. Bragg was only 25.

New metal, new wavelength

Interference of X-rays can be produced by passing them through very narrow slits, and techniques using special mechanically produced diffraction gratings have been developed. By projecting the X-rays at a small angle of incidence, the grating lines appear very close together and diffraction occurs even at the very short wavelengths of X-rays. This method has given values of X-ray wavelengths which confirm Bragg's Law based on the calculated dimensions of the crystal.

Using the X-ray spectrometer, the Braggs investigated X-ray wavelengths from a tube whose target could be changed from one metal to another, and in which the voltage across the plates could be varied. For relatively low tube voltages, they found that a range or spectrum of X-ray wavelengths is produced which ends abruptly at the short wavelength end. Increasing the tube voltage moves this cut-off point to a shorter wavelength. At a certain high value of voltage, in addition to the broad X-ray spectrum the tube produces strong X-rays at definite wavelengths.

They found that changing the metal of the target from, say, copper to nickel and repeating the experiment produces another broad spectrum and again at high voltages a set of strong X-ray lines. But the lines for nickel have different wavelengths from those for copper. These strong X-ray lines are called *characteristic X-rays* because they are characteristic of the target metal.

Shortly after W. H. Bragg's observations, the origin of characteristic X-rays was linked with the production of characteristic light wavelengths by certain

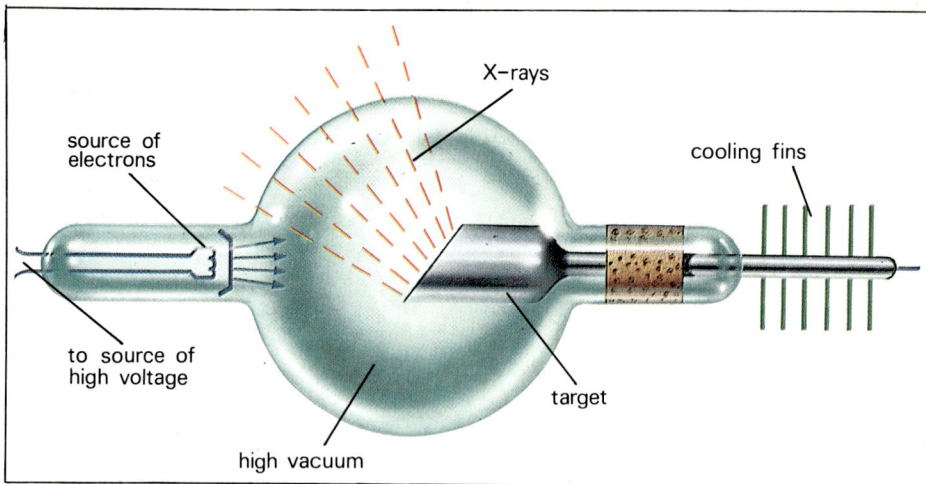

A stream of electrons 'fired' from a source of high voltage, thus carrying a large quantity of energy, strikes a metal target, *above*, and X-rays are given off. The vacuum is to prevent dissipation of the electrons' energy through collision with air molecules. This X-ray photo of a rattlesnake digesting a prairie dog, *right*, offers invaluable information to the biologist.

elements. (For example, sodium produces yellow light, neon produces red light, and so on.) From a knowledge of quantum theory these can be explained. The high-speed electrons falling on to the target have a certain energy. While this energy is relatively low (that is, at low tube voltages), the electrons collide with the heavy target atoms and are scattered about. At each collision they lose energy which is radiated in the form of X-rays.

Since they lose various amounts of energy at each collision, the X-ray wavelengths produced are many, and a broad X-ray spectrum is formed. But at a certain tube voltage, the electrons have sufficient energy to eject other electrons from the innermost orbits of the target atoms. The spaces left by the ejected electrons are filled by electrons falling from higher orbits, each releasing a definite quantum of energy in doing so. According to quantum theory, the quantum of energy is related to the frequency of the energy released. So for a particular target atom,

X-rays of definite wavelength are emitted. A different target atom has a different arrangement of orbits, and so the quanta of energy involved are also different, leading to characteristic X-rays of definite wavelengths.

The important investigations into the structures of crystals using X-rays were begun by M. von Laue (who in 1912 first predicted diffraction of X-rays by crystals) and continued by the Braggs. The way in which a simple crystal such as that of common salt diffracts X-rays was explained by W. H. Bragg in connection with his X-ray spectrometer. He considered that X-rays are scattered by each of the crystal atoms. In any direction, the scattered X-rays will add together only if their waves are in phase (in step). If we consider one crystal plane (in a cubic crystal there will be three sets of such planes at right angles), the scattered X-rays from that plane will be in phase for one direction only. This direction has the same relationship to the angle of incidence as do the

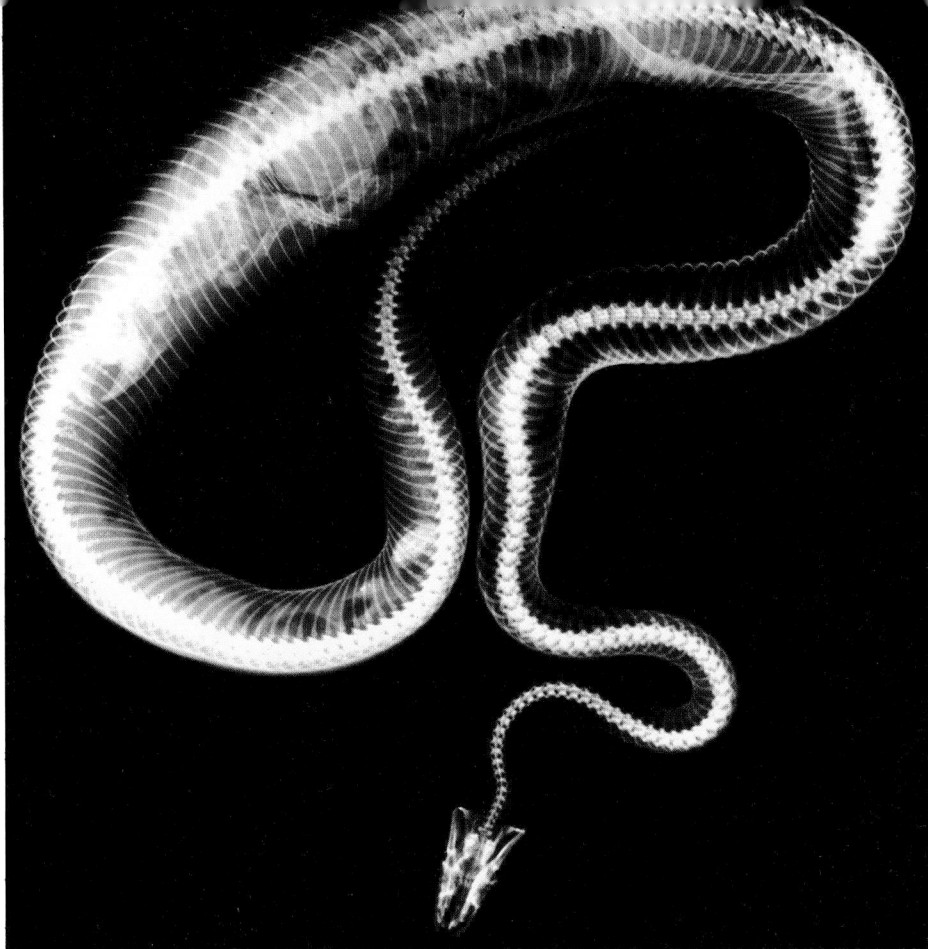

incident and reflected light rays at a mirror. If the same effect occurs for the many crystal planes lying beneath the one considered, and if all the reflected rays are in phase, there will be a strong overall reflection in one direction only. This direction depends on the wavelength of the X-rays, the angle of incidence, and the spacing between the crystal planes, and is predicted by Bragg's Law.

If the crystal is rotated and other crystal planes used, the shape and volume of the crystal can be found and the number of atoms in the crystal determined. With extremely simple crystals, the numbers of atoms can be found by calculation without using the spectrometer; but for complex crystals, this method is the basis of the most useful way of analysing them. Techniques developed by W.L. Bragg have enabled scientists to measure even the structures of organic crystals. Other important X-ray crystal studies include those of the structures of metals and new alloys, and of organic fibres.

Shadow pictures

The more familiar applications of X-rays use their penetrating properties. Unlike light, which is stopped by even a flimsy

X-rays can probe behind the painted surface of a masterpiece to reveal important secrets. The painting of St Michael, *left*, by Piero della Francesca, now hanging in the National Gallery in London, was suspected to be part of a lost five-panel altarpiece prepared for the Church of St Agostino in Italy in the mid-1400s. An X-ray revealed a tell-tale piece of drapery in the lower right-hand corner, as in the cleaned painting, *right*. Four of the five panels have now been located, and the art world is now on the lookout for the fifth to complete the work.

material such as paper, X-rays can penetrate quite dense materials. In passing through a material, the intensity or 'brightness' of the X-rays is progressively reduced (like light passing through cloudy water). Since different materials reduce the intensity at a different rate, X-rays passed through, say, the human body will be more strongly absorbed by bone than by the surrounding flesh. By placing a photographic plate behind the body, a 'shadow' X-ray picture may be produced. Tissues which are or have been diseased, for instance the scar tissue left in the lungs after tuberculosis, show up darker than the surrounding tissues because they absorb slightly more X-rays. Additional techniques, such as the barium sulphate meal used for X-raying the stomach, are used to make soft tissues show up on X-ray photographs. In this example, an ulcer would absorb some of the barium sulphate and would show up strongly on the X-ray plate.

X-rays are also used in industry; for example, to examine metal objects encapsulated in plastic, or to 'see' through an opaque substance as in the locating of grids in thermionic valves. Important too are X-ray techniques for detecting flaws in metals. Although a metal casting or a machined component may appear sound, it can contain an internal flaw which seriously affects its strength. If X-ray photographs could not be used, the only other ways of easily detecting the flaw would involve destroying the component. For example, hitting a small casting with a big hammer detects flaws, but it smashes the casting.

The dangers of X-irradiation to the body are now recognized, and people who work with X-ray machines are well protected by lead shielding. Until about 15 years ago, it was common to see X-ray machines in shops to aid in fitting shoes, especially for children. These machines projected X-rays up through the foot and on to a fluorescent screen. If they were used frequently, there may have been some danger, so most of them have now been withdrawn. The effects of small doses of X-rays on tissues are negligible. But prolonged exposure can have serious consequences and ultimately destroys the tissues. Important too is the effect of X-rays on genes and chromosomes. Mutated genes can have disastrous effects if they are passed on in reproduction. For this reason, X-rays are rarely used on women in early pregnancy, although in some cases the slight risk may be justified by the essential information an X-ray examination can provide.

Medical science has turned the damaging effects of X-irradiation to good use. X-ray therapy is an important part of the treatment for malignant diseases such as cancer. Using a very carefully directed and controlled X-ray source, the affected tissues can be destroyed, and the cell-multiplying effects caused by certain kinds of cancer arrested.

The quantum explanation of the energy associated with X-rays showed that, as the wavelength of the radiation becomes shorter, so the energy becomes greater. Short wavelength X-rays therefore have more penetrating power than do longer wavelengths. Very short wavelength X-rays are very penetrating, and closely resemble their near neighbours in the electro-magnetic spectrum, gamma rays.

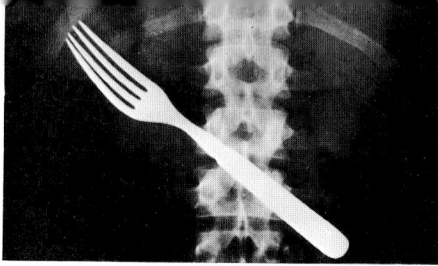

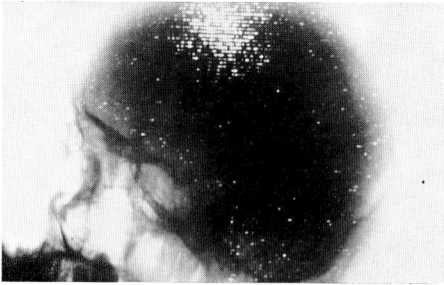

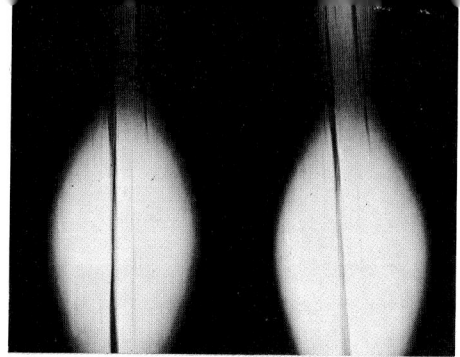

Gamma rays have many of the properties of X-rays (they can be diffracted by crystals, they affect photographic plates and cause feeble fluorescence, they pass through metals, and so on); their origin is different. Characteristic emission of light and X-rays is due to electrons jumping between energy levels. Gamma radiation is produced by activity originating in the nucleus of the atom. It occurs when the nucleus adjusts itself from one 'excited' state to another. It is interesting that the quantum theory again satisfactorily explains the mechanism: the nucleus can settle in only certain energy states and in moving from one state to another of lower energy, a quantum of gamma radiation is emitted. The nucleus gets into a position from which it must change in this way after the emission of a beta particle (an electron).

Gamma radiation

Gamma rays can also be responsible for the emission of X-rays. As a gamma ray leaves the nucleus, it passes through the electron orbits of the atom and may eject an electron from one of them. The conditions are then similar to those in an X-ray tube, and another electron falls into the vacant space, emitting a characteristic X-ray quantum. In this way, a radioactive material emitting gamma radiation may also produce X-rays. This phenomenon can be used for analysing mixtures of elements. If the mixture is made radioactive, its X-ray spectrum can be examined and, from the characteristic lines present, the elements in the mixture can be identified.

When X-rays were first discovered, many people were quite apprehensive. However, research has stripped them of their mystery and technology has put them to useful work. X-rays have become an important part of our daily life.

A man came to a doctor complaining of stomach pains. An X-ray, *top left,* revealed the cause. He had swallowed a fork. Bowling pins, *top right,* are regularly X-rayed to detect flaws. Brain tumours, a more serious kind of flaw, are also revealed by X-ray, with the aid of radio-isotopes, *above left.* Numerous lives have been saved in this way. Study of X-rays and other such phenomena led to the need for protection. This make-shift lead mask, *below,* is an example of the primitive protective devices the early researchers had to fashion for themselves. It is an exhibit at the Röntgen Museum in Remscheid, West Germany, where Röntgen was born.

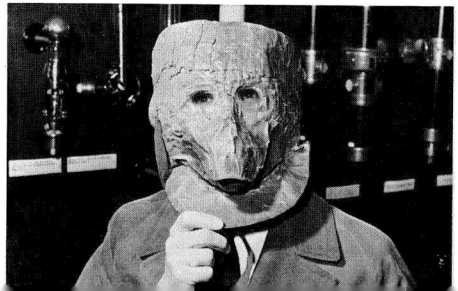

Dark energy and light

Between the longest radio waves and gamma rays of the shortest wavelength is a broad spectrum of radiant energy. At one point it is punctuated by a narrow 'rainbow' of light waves.

TO MOST PEOPLE, light is what happens when the sun comes up at dawn, when we strike a match or set fire to a candle-wick or when we turn on an electric lamp. In the sun, the light comes from a nuclear reaction similar to the one which takes place when a hydrogen bomb explodes. In a candle, light comes from a chemical reaction as the wax of the candle burns. And in an electric lamp, light comes from a metal filament that is heated by the electric current until it becomes incandescent.

All these sources of light are hot. So we would expect light to be closely related to heat; and like heat, light is a kind of energy. In fact, if we take a piece of metal and make it hotter and hotter, it begins by emitting heat. Then it becomes red-, yellow- and finally white-hot, dazzling to the eye because it is emitting light.

Radiation and the hot mouse

To the scientist, light is a form of *electromagnetic radiation*. There are many such forms of radiation ranging from radio waves, microwaves used in radar and heat rays through to light and X-rays and cosmic rays. They all take the form of waves (radio waves have the longest wavelength and cosmic rays the shortest). They make up a continuous spectrum of electromagnetic radiation with visible light forming just a small part of the spectrum in the middle. Or put another way, light is the part of the electromagnetic spectrum to which our eyes are sensitive.

Human beings cannot see other types of electromagnetic radiation, although they can be detected. For example, we can 'feel' heat rays and we can take photographs using X-rays. The kind of radiation with a wavelength slightly longer than red light is called *infra-red*. We can take photographs using infra-red radiation and obtain aerial and satellite photographs of great clarity, because infra-red rays easily penetrate thin cloud and haze.

Although we cannot 'see' infra-red rays, there is evidence that some animals can. Some rattle-snakes (or pit vipers) have pit-shaped organs on the sides of their heads. By means of these organs, the snakes seem to be able in pitch darkness to detect any object or animal that is a few degrees warmer than its surroundings. For example, a mouse sitting absolutely still in the blackness of the desert night emits feeble infra-red radiation because of the warmth of its body. A rattle-snake seems to be able to detect this radiation, use it to estimate the range and direction of the mouse and unerringly strike at it.

Other animals have their range of light sensitivity shifted towards shorter wavelengths, beyond blue light into the *ultra-violet*. For example, bees and ants are completely blind in red light but can see perfectly well by ultra-violet light. We can also take photographs by such light and our bodies are slightly sensitive to the ultra-violet rays in sunlight – they cause sun tan.

The part of the electromagnetic spectrum which human beings can see is called visible light. There is nothing mysterious about infra-red and ultra-violet radiations, which are invisible to us. It is just that they are outside the range of sensitivity of the receptors in the human eye. They may be 'visible' to animals and to photographic emulsions.

Light is a type of wave motion characterized by such quantities as wavelength, frequency and amplitude. Wavelength is the distance between successive crests of waves and, since this is very small for visible light, is generally measured in angstrom units (Å) or millimicrons (mμ). An angstrom unit equals a hundred-millionth of a centimetre, and a milli-micron equals a ten-millionth of a centimetre. Visible light has wavelengths between about 390 mμ (violet) and 700 mμ (red).

Frequency is the number of wave pulses emitted in one second. Since light travels through space at a constant velocity of 300,000 kilometres a second (symbol *c*), frequency equals *c* divided by wavelength. Amplitude is half the vertical distance from a crest to a trough (Vol. I, p. 369). Large amplitude means bright light, small amplitude means dull light.

In 1666, the British mathematician and physicist Sir Isaac Newton (1642–1727) discovered that when a beam of sunlight is passed through a prism, the light is split up into bands of coloured lights called a *spectrum*. If the coloured lights are mixed in the correct proportions, white light again results. Lights of different colours differ in wavelength, red light having a longer wavelength than blue light.

How does a prism separate white light, which consists of a mixture of many wavelengths, into the various components of

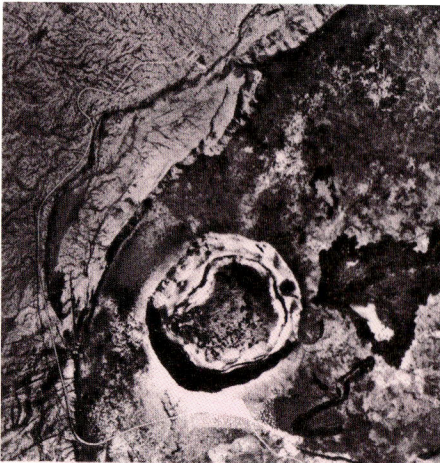

Heat rays invisible to the eye pour up from volcanoes in Hawaii. These are the infra-red rays, lower in frequency than red rays in the visible spectrum, longer in wavelength than

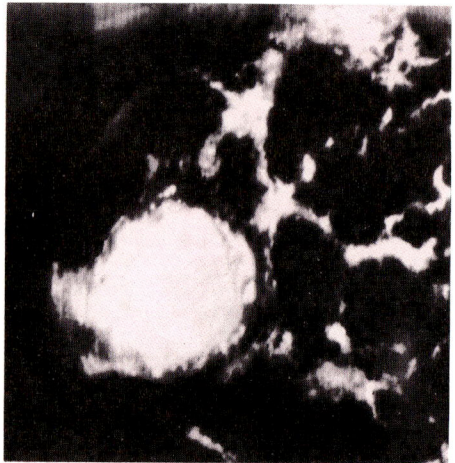

visible light. Specially sensitive photographic film records this radiation in the picture *above*. Penetrating mist and darkness, the infra-red photographer can find enemy transport by night.

the spectrum? To answer this question we need to understand *refraction* of light. As we have seen, light always travels at the same velocity in a single medium, such as air. But in different media, light travels at different velocities. If the second medium is optically more dense than the first (as in the case of a ray entering a piece of glass), the speed of the light is decreased and the ray changes direction slightly. The light ray is effectively and abruptly bent from its original path, and this bending is called refraction.

The effect of refraction can easily be seen by looking at a stick dipping into a pool of water or a straw in a glass of water. That part of the stick under the water appears to be bent; this is because light rays reflected from the immersed part of the stick are refracted as they leave the water, making our eyes 'see' the stick in a different position.

Bending the beam

Different materials refract light to different extents, and the property of a transparent material which determines the extent of refraction is called its *refractive index*. Refractive index is the ratio of the velocity of light in air to the velocity of light in the transparent material. Since light always travels slower in the denser medium, the refractive index is always greater than 1. For example, light travels through water at about three-quarters of its velocity in air, and the refractive index of water is about 1·3.

Glass lenses work by refraction. Rays of light passing through the curved surface of a lens are refracted and, depending on the shape of the lens, emerge travelling in a new direction. For example, with a simple *convex* lens (which has both its curved faces bulging outwards), a parallel bundle of light rays passing through the lens converge and are brought to a focus. The bending of the rays as they pass through the lens is due to refraction.

If the clouds in the sky are sailing from right to left, they will move from left to right in the mirror image of the glass wall, *above.* Reflection reverses the picture of the real world.

Returning now to the glass prism, we can see how a beam of white light is split into a spectrum. The beam of white light consists of a mixture of wavelengths, and each wavelength is refracted to a slightly different extent as it passes through the prism.

Spectra are studied by means of an

instrument called a spectroscope. It has a system of lenses to produce a narrow, parallel beam of light; a turntable on which a prism is mounted; and a telescope for viewing the spectrum. The telescope may be replaced by a camera for photographing the spectrum, and the instrument is then known as a spectrograph.

Like other waves, light can exhibit the phenomenon of *interference*. When two light waves of the same wavelength overlap, they may interfere. If the waves are *in phase* (in step), the crests of one wave coincide with the crests of the other. As a result, the amplitude of the combined wave is increased and with it the intensity of the light. But if the waves are out of phase, the crests of one coincide with the troughs of the other, the waves cancel, and the amplitude and intensity are decreased. If the interfering light waves fall on to a screen, waves in phase produce bright bands of light on the screen and waves out of phase produce dark bands.

The rainbow on the bubble

Interference bands may be seen when light is reflected from an extremely thin film of transparent material or from a thin film of air trapped between two pieces of glass. In the case of a thin film of material, such as the skin of a soap bubble or a thin film of oil or petrol on water, interference produces brilliant colours of the rainbow. Some light is reflected from the front surface of the film, and some passes through the front surface and is reflected inside the thickness of the film from the back surface. Since the film is so thin, rays reflected from the back surface have to travel just a small distance farther, and some of them may emerge out of phase with the rays reflected from the front surface. The interference bands are coloured because only light of a certain wavelength, and hence of a certain colour, will be exactly out of phase for a particular thickness of

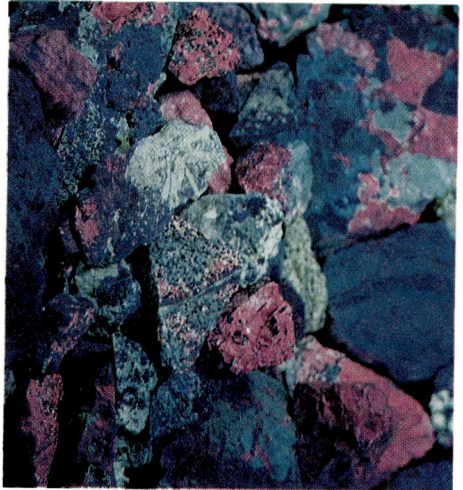

When you, raindrops and the sun are in line, a rainbow appears, *above*. Light bends as it enters a raindrop, is reflected inside, and bends again as it leaves — splitting into colours. Fluorescent substances, such as the crystals *below*, emit visible long-wave light when invisible short-wave ultra-violet light falls on them. This quality forms the basis of flourescent lighting.

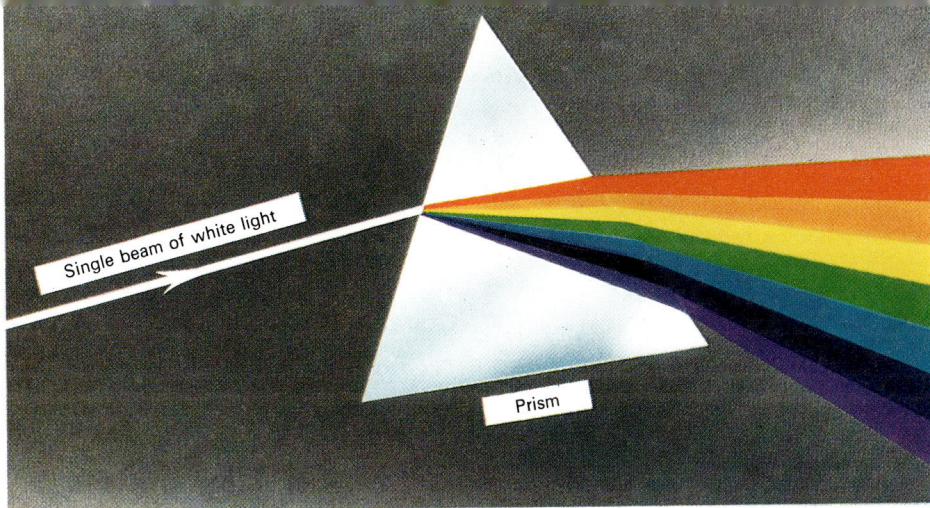

Single beam of white light

Prism

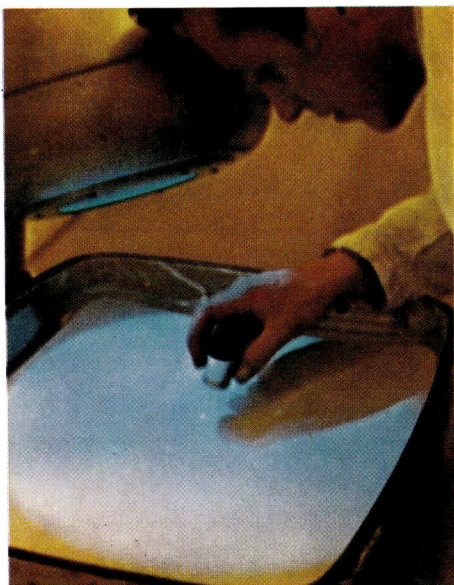

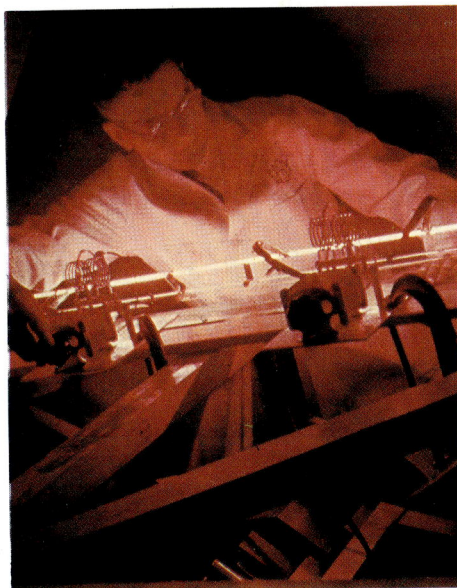

Top, white light is a mixture of many wavelengths. It moves faster in air than in glass. The effect of slowing it is to *refract*, or bend it. The glass prism refracts each wavelength by different amounts, and so splits the light. *Left*, ultra-violet reveals imperfections on the screen of a colour television set. *Right*, a light beam that can drill holes in diamonds is created in the device called a laser (light amplification by stimulated emission of radiation).

film. This colour is therefore missing from the reflected light and we see only the remaining spectral colours.

Thin films of air between two pieces of glass give interference bands known as Newton's rings. In white light the rings are coloured, and may be seen when photographic transparencies are mounted between two sheets of glass for projection.

Why is the colour of molten metal yellow, not green or blue? The explanation is that heat and light are both made up of wavelengths on the same electromagnetic spectrum. Yellow light, red light and heat rays are close neighbours.

If monochromatic light is used – that is, light of a single colour (and hence a single wavelength) – Newton's rings appear merely as alternate light and dark bands with no coloured fringes.

Coloured interference fringes can also be produced by using a point source of white light to cast shadows of an object on to a screen. These fringes are due to a slight bending of the light rays as they pass the obstacle casting the shadow; this bending is called *diffraction*. Some rays are bent more than others – that is, some travel a little farther. If the waves become out of phase, interference occurs and fringes are formed.

Diffraction is easier to understand if we consider a coherent source of mono-chromatic light passing through a very narrow slit (monochromatic light consists of waves of the same wavelength; coherent waves are perfectly in step). Light

passing through the slit on to a screen produces a series of light and dark inter-ference bands. With two narrow slits close together instead of one, the inter-ference bands are brighter and sharper. With several slits, the bands become even finer.

A diffraction grating consists of a piece of glass with thousands of very fine lines scribed on it close together. The unscribed parts of the glass act as very narrow slits and diffract light passing through them. The first diffraction gratings were made by Joseph von Fraunhofer (1820) and Henry Rowland (1882).

Light through a grating

As we have seen, different wavelengths of light are diffracted to different extents. So that if white light is passed through a dif-fraction grating, it is split up into a spectrum in the same way as is light passed through a prism. A diffraction grating can be used instead of a prism in a spectroscope.

Ruling fine lines close together on the surface of a glass or metal mirror pro-duces a *reflection* grating. This grating behaves in much the same way as does a normal diffraction grating and produces spectra. But if the ruled mirror is also cor-rectly curved, it will focus its own spectral lines without the need for glass lenses. This technique is used in spectrometers for studying ultra-violet light, which is absorbed by glass. Coloured interference fringes may be seen when white light is reflected from a finely ruled or grooved surface, such as a long-playing gramo-phone record, which acts as a reflection grating.

All the properties of light described in this article can be explained by regarding light as existing as waves. But physicists have not always thought that this is so, and since the 1900s new ideas have been put forward about the nature of light.

Originally, physicists thought that light

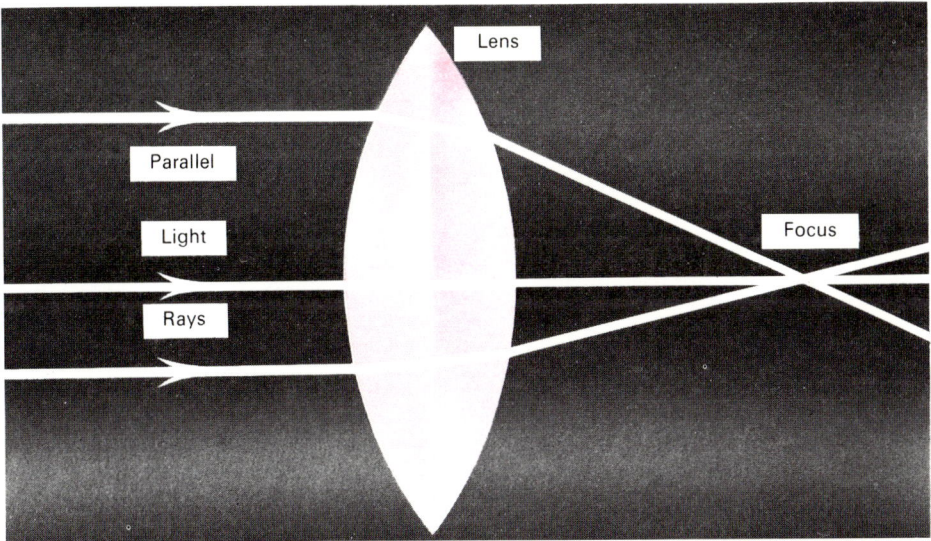

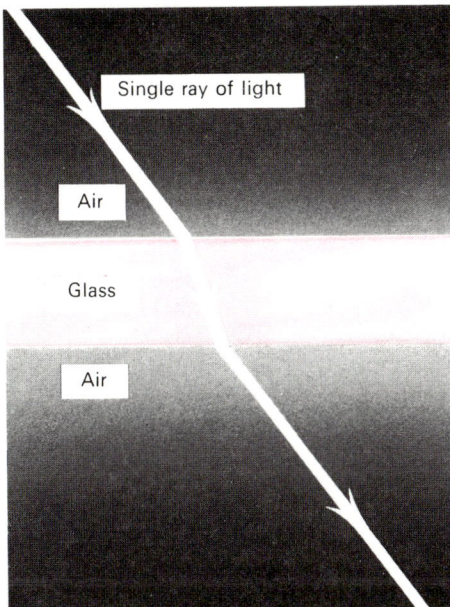

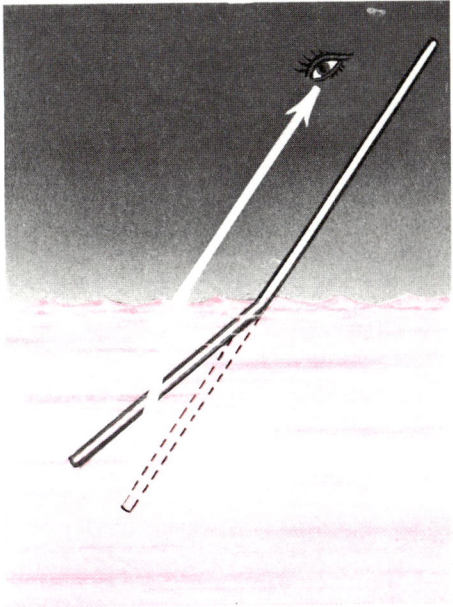

Top, parallel rays of light bend towards a single point – the focus – after passing through a double convex lens. *Above left,* the velocity of light changes when it passes from one optical medium to another. The decrease in speed changes the direction of the ray. *Above right,* the effect of refraction, or bending of light can be seen by looking at a stick in water. The stick seems bent.

consists of tiny particles called *corpuscles*. Newton was a champion of the corpuscular theory, and he developed explanations for all common phenomena of light in terms of it. Light sources were supposed to shoot out corpuscles in all directions at great speeds. In reflection, the corpuscles were assumed to bounce off an object such as a mirror rather as a ball bounces off a wall – or, rather, as a bullet richochets off a tank. But Newton had great difficulty in accounting for the refraction of light as it passes from a less dense to a more dense medium. To do so, he assumed that the speed of the corpuscles *increased* inside the denser medium. Experimental measurements, the first of which were made by Foucault in 1853, showed that the opposite was true: light travels more slowly in a denser medium.

Energy in packets

Even while Newton was elaborating the corpuscular theory, other scientists such as Robert Hooke (1635–1703) and Christian Huygens (1629–95) were suggesting that light is a form of wave motion. One of the convincing arguments for the alternative theory was its satisfactory explanation of refraction.

Then at the end of the last century, the German physicist Max Planck introduced his famous *quantum theory,* which postulates that there is a fundamental unit of energy, called a quantum. According to this theory, radiant energy such as light does not consist of continuous waves but of separate 'packets' of energy, called *photons* in the case of light. In certain circumstances, photons behave as if they were particles, in agreement with Louis de Broglie's hypothesis (1924) that all forms of radiant energy can be considered to be made up of particles, and that all fundamental particles can be considered to exist as waves. The amount of energy 'carried' by a photon depends on the wavelength (or frequency) of light.

The theories about light seem to have turned full circle. Neither Newton nor Huygens was completely right – but, according to modern views, neither was completely wrong.

In the future, it may well be that the intensely powerful beams of lasers, which show up one million times brighter than the brilliance of our sun, could well be used to transmit interstellar messages. But light-borne conversations across space will always be lengthy affairs. Even at the speed of light, a reply from Alpha Centauri, our nearest star, could not be received until eight and a half years after a question reached it from Earth.

Index